Montgomery, Alabama, John W. A. Sanford

The Code of the City of Montgomery

Prepared in pursuance of an order of the City Council of Montgomery

Montgomery, Alabama, John W. A. Sanford

The Code of the City of Montgomery
Prepared in pursuance of an order of the City Council of Montgomery

ISBN/EAN: 9783337302177

Printed in Europe, USA, Canada, Australia, Japan

Cover: Foto ©Suzi / pixelio.de

More available books at **www.hansebooks.com**

CITY OF MONTGOMERY,

PREPARED IN PURSUANCE OF AN

Order of the City Council of Montgomery.

────── •• ──────

BY JOHN W. A. SANFORD.

── ── • ──────

ERRATA.

On page 30, § 18, for "which," read which.
On page 31, § 24, for "cach," read each.
On page 45, § 102, for "such," read such.
On page 47, § 113, for "fighing," read fighting.
On page 45, § 114, omit the word "nine."
On page 57, § 167, for "office," read office.
On page 63, § 199, for "council," read council.
On page 66, § 220, for "licence," read license.
On page 74, § 266, for "ea," read every.
On page 78, § 293, for "moret han," read more than.
On page 87, § 346, for "informer," read informer.

ERRATA IN MARGINAL NOTES.

On page 29, § 17, for "approbrious," read opprobrious.
On page 29, § 27, for "if any," read if no.
On page 34, § 42, for "artesion," read artesian.
On page 37, § 61, for "agast," read against.
On page 50, § 133, for "foregoin," read foregoing.
On page 51, § 134, for "lectues," read lecture.
On page 56, § 164, for "fires," read fences.
On page 64, § 206, for "pedling," read peddling.
On page 67, § 224, for "licenses," read licenses.
On page 75, § 271, for "removrl," read removal.
On page 79, § 301, for "patrollers," read patrol.
On page 80, § 303, for "ten," read two.
On page 82, § 311, for "retaile," read retailer.
On page 95, § 396, for "upon," read issue.
On page 99, § 418, for "wharfinfier," read wharfinger.
On page 99, § 419, for "ratee," read rates.

AN ACT

To Incorporate the City of Montgomery, approved December 23d, 1837.

SECTION 1.—*Be it enacted by the Senate and House of Representatives of the State of Alabama, in General Assembly convened—*

That the town of Montgomery, in said State, shall hereafter be called the city of Montgomery, and that the said town or city shall include within its corporate limits, fractional section twelve, in township sixteen, and range seventeen, East of the Alabama river, and so much of the North-East quarter of section thirteen, in township sixteen and range seventeen, as has been heretofore surveyed and laid out in lots of a size less than one acre; and so much of the North-West quarter of section seven in the last named township and range, as has been heretofore surveyed, and laid out in lots of a size less than one acre; and also the fractional section twelve, in township sixteen, East of the Alabama river; the North-East quarter of section thirteen, in township sixteen and range seventeen; the North-West quarter of section eighteen in township sixteen and range eighteen; the South West quarter of section seven, in township sixteen and range eighteen; the North-West quarter of section seven, in township sixteen and range eighteen; the West halt of the South-East quarter of section sev-

Incorporation.

Amended by an Act January 24, 1839.

Amended by Act Jan. 13th, 1844.

en, in township sixteen, and range eighteen; and a piece of land containing nine and thirty-five hundredths acres, by Amerson's Survey, situated immediately East of that point of said city known as Scott's Town, and inclosed and used as a burying ground; the West half of the North-East quarter of section seven, township sixteen range eighteen;

Amended by Act, Feb. 13, 1850.

and the inhabitants whereof shall be a body corporate, and that the Mayor and Aldermen of said city, when elected and qualified, as hereinafter directed, shall be named and styled "The City Council of Montgomery," and by that name may purchase, receive, hold, or let, sell, grant, alien, or assure property, real and personal, and sue and be sued, plead and be impleaded, and to do and perform any other acts incident to bodies corporate, to have a common seal which may be changed at pleasure, and that the jurisdiction shall extend to and include all the lands above described, and all the Alabama river opposite to said fractional section twelve.

May purchase real or personal property, sue and be sued.

Seal.

Jurisdiction of the city.

Amended by an Act, Nov. 23rd, 1853.

SECTION 2.—*Be it further enacted,* That the corporation limits of said city of Montgomery be, and the same are divided into six Wards, as follows:

The city divided into six Wards.

All that part of said city lying South-West of Commerce street, North-West of Montgomery street, and North of Clayton street, shall form the First Ward, and shall be known and styled as Ward number one;

Ward No. 1.

And all that part of said city lying South-East of Montgomery street, South of Clayton street, and West of Court street, shall form the Second Ward, and shall be known and styled as Ward number two;

Ward No. 2.

And all that part of said city lying East of Court street, South of Market street, and West of Law-

Ward No. 3.

rence street, shall form the Third Ward, and shall be known and styled as Ward number three;

And all that part of said city lying East of Lawrence street, South of Market and South Market streets, shall form the Fourth Ward, and shall be known and styled as Ward number four; Ward No. 4.

And all that part of said city lying North of Market and South Market streets, and East of Perry street, shall form the Fifth Ward, and shall be known and styled as Ward number five; Ward No. 5.

And all that part of said city lying North of Market street, and North-East of Commerce, and West of Perry street, shall form the Sixth Ward, and shall be known as Ward number six; Ward No. 6.

And each of said Wards, numbers one, two, three, four, five and six, shall, and is hereby declared entitled to two Aldermen, who shall reside in the same, and who shall be elected annually by the qualified electors thereof; and an election shall be held in each Ward on the first Monday in December in each and every year, for a Mayor, who shall reside within the limits of said city, and two Aldermen for each Ward; and the person having the greatest number of votes for Mayor in said city shall be Mayor, and the two persons in each Ward having the greatest number of votes for Aldermen, shall be Aldermen for such Ward; but if two or more persons have an equal number of votes for Mayor, the Aldermen shall determine who shall be Mayor; and if no two persons in any ward shall have a higher number of votes than any other person, the Mayor and Aldermen shall determine who shall be Aldermen for that Ward, the one having the highest number always being one. The said Mayor and Aldermen shall hold their office until

Each of the Wards shall be entitled to two Aldermen.

Act Nov. 23, 1853.

Election shall be held on first Monday in December of every year.

In case of a tie for Mayor

for Aldermen.

the next succeeding election after their election or appointment, and until their successors are duly elected and qualified ; if a vacancy occur in the office of Mayor or Aldermen by death, resignation, removal, or otherwise, such vacancies shall be filled by the Mayor and Aldermen, or by the Aldermen, as the case may be ; the Aldermen shall judge of the qualification of the Mayor, and the Mayor and Aldermen shall judge of the qualification of each Alderman.

Term of office.

Vacancies, how filled.

Who shall decide elections.

SECTION 3.—*And be it further enacted,* That the Intendant and Council of the town of Montgomery shall appoint at least two discreet and respectable freeholders or lot holders in each Ward, who shall be managers of the next election, and said city Council shall make such appointments thereafter. All white male citizens of this State, above the age of twenty-one years, who shall have resided within said city six months immediately preceding an election, who shall have paid a poll tax for the municipal year, shall be qualified electors for Mayor and Aldermen ; and no person shall be elegible to the office of Mayor or Aldermen, unless, in addition to the qualification of elector, he shall have resided in said city one year next preceding an election, and be a freeholder or lot holder in said city : *Provided,* that so much of this section as provides the payment of taxes as a qualification of an elector, or Mayor or Alderman, shall not apply to persons living at the next election on the above described lands, and out of the limits of the town of Montgomery.

Two freeholders to be appointed.

Qualification of voters for city officers.

Amended by Act, Nov. 29, 1859.

Qualification of Mayor or Aldermen.

Proviso.

SECTION 4.—*And be it further enacted,* That the said Mayor and Aldermen, shall severally, before they enter upon the duties of their office, in addi-

Oath of office.

tion to the oath prescribed for civil officers of the State, make and subscribe an affidavit that they will endeavor to prevent and punish all tumultuous and riotous assemblies, assaults and batteries, gaming, keeping gaming houses, and all other public offences and violations of the laws of the State and ordinances of said city; and will faithfully, to the best of their skill and judgment, execute their office without favor or partiality; which affidavit shall be filed in the office of the Clerk of said city.

SECTION 5.—*And be it further enacted*, That the said Mayor and Aldermen, in Council assembled, shall have power and authority to pass by-laws and ordinances necessary and proper to prevent contagious and infectious diseases from being introduced into said city, and to preserve the health thereof; to prevent and remove all nuisances at the expense of the person causing such nuisance, or upon whose property it may be found; to license. tax, regulate and restrain theatrical amusements and shows; to restrain and prohibit gaming, and keeping gaming houses and houses of ill fame; to establish night watches and day watches, and patrols, and to appoint leaders and captains thereof; to make, alter, and ascertain new streets and alleys; to clean and keep in repair the streets and alleys; to regulate the stationing, moving and anchorage of steamboats, and other boats and craft within their jurisdiction; to have a general control and superintendance over the wharf, wharfages, ferry, ferriages, public springs and wells; to establish necessary inspections; to erect and regulate markets and the assize of bread; to regulate the conveyance of water from the vicinity into the said city; to regulate the sales at auctions, and to appoint auctioneers: *Provided* the same shall not extend to sales under execution by

To pass by-laws to prevent contagious diseases to preserve the health, remove nuisances, restrain exhibitions, gaming. houses of ill fame establish watches patrol &c. new streets repair streets, regulate boats &c. superintend the wharf, ferry and wells, regulate markets, appoint auctioneers.

Proviso.

order of court, or by executors or administrators;
to erect public scale houses, with proper scales,
weights and measures; and to appoint weighers
and measurers to weigh and measure in case of dis-
agreement between buyer and seller; to license
and regulate wagons, carts and drays, and such
hacks and carriages, running from one part of the
said city to another part for hire; and generally to
pass such by-laws and ordinances not contrary to
the Constitution and laws of this State, as said
Mayor and Aldermen shall from time to time deem
necessary and proper to carry into effect the true
intent and meaning of this act, and the same to enforce, alter and repeal.

The qualified voters for Mayor and Aldermen in
the city of Montgomery shall be authorized to vote
for and elect, annually, a Clerk, at the same time,
and under the same regulations which are now prescribed for the election of Mayor and Aldermen:
Provided, nevertheless, that the Clerk so elected,
for maladministration in office, shall be subject to
removal by the City Council; and all vacancies
thus created shall be filled by the City Council.—
The said Mayor and Aldermen shall have power to
appoint and remove at pleasure Treasurer and such
number of Marshals and other officers as they
may deem necessary and proper, and require such
bond and security as they may deem necessary, and
to annex such fees and salaries to their several offices, and to impose such fines for neglect of duty in
office, not exceeding one hundred dollars, as they
may deem necessary; the said Mayor and Aldermen are also empowered to lay such fines, not exceeding fifty dollars, for breach or breaches of their
by-laws and ordinances, as they may deem proper,
and to enforce and collect the same in such manner

Regulate weights and measures, license carts wagons, &c.

To pass laws not contrary to the Constitution and laws of the State.

Amended Act, Jan. 4, 1843.

The Clerk shall be e-lected by the citizens.

The Mayor and Alder-men may appoint Treasurer, Marshal, & such other officers as may be ne-cessary.

Fees & sal-aries.

Neglect of duty finable

Fines.

as may be prescribed by ordinance, by execution against the person or property, or committing to jail, as they may deem necessary or proper, which fines shall be appropriated in such manner as the said City Council may prescribe ; *Provided*, that this act and all the by-laws, and ordinances of said city shall at all times be subject to revision or repeal by the General Assembly.

To enforce by execution against the person or property.

Proviso.

SECTION 6.—*And be it further enacted*, That the said Mayor and Aldermen, shall have power and authority for the ordinary current expenses of said city, to assess, levy and collect annually, a tax on real estate, not exceeding one-half of one per cent. on the cash value thereof, and no more in any one year, and the City Council of Montgomery shall not contract any debt or incur any liability for, or on account of the city of Montgomery, which is not to be paid out of the ordinary current revenue of the year in which said debt or liability is contracted or incurred, and any such debt or liability attempted to be contracted or incurred by the said City Council, in violation of the foregoing provisions shall be void, as against the city of Montgomery. The Mayor and Aldermen shall have power and authority to pass laws for the assessment, levy, and collection of taxes not exceeding the following rates :

To assess and collect taxes.

Amended by act Feb. 15, 1856.

A poll tax, not exceeding two dollars on each white male inhabitant above twenty-one years of age : *Provided*, He shall have resided in said city two months immediately preceding the time said tax shall be levied ; on each slave over ten and under fifty years of age, not exceeding one dollar ; on every free negro or mulatto, who shall reside in said city, not exceeding ten dollars ; a tax on all pleasure carriages, gigs, chairs and sulkies, not ex-

Poll tax.

Tax on slaves, free negro or mulatto, carriages, carts, wagons. &c.

ceeding one per cent on the value thereof; on every cart, dray, wagon and other vehicle, used for the transportation of goods and commodities from one part of said city to another for hire, a tax not exceeding twenty dollars; on every retailer of spirituous liquors, a tax not less than forty, nor more than five hundred dollars; on every vendor of goods, wares and merchandise, drugs and medicines, or either of them, a tax not exceeding twenty-five dollars per annum; on all goods sold at auction, a tax not exceeding one per cent. on amount of sales, or not exceeding fifty dollars per annum; and for each livery or sale stable, fifty dollars; lottery offices or agencies two hundred dollars; insurance offices, foreign or otherwise, fifty dollars; free banks or bank agencies, one hundred dollars; negro traders or brokers, one hundred dollars; all persons buying cotton on commission, or otherwise, twenty-five dollars; hotels, fifty dollars; theatres, shows, or other exhibitions, five dollars for each day's performance or exhibition, lectures when an admission fee is charged except for charitable or benevolent purposes, five dollars for each lecture; circuses for each day's or night's performances, twenty dollars; peddlers, thirty-five dollars; lawyers, doctors, dentists, and daguerrian artists, five dollars each; billiard, pool, bagatelle, or other tables kept for playing, one hundred dollars each; ten pin alleys or alleys with any other number of pins, fifty dollars; restaurants, fifty dollars each; concerts for profit, five dollars each; auctioneers, fifty dollars; warehouses for the storage of cotton, one hundred dollars; public scales, twenty-five dollars each; furniture, silver-plated ware, above the value of five hundred dollars, one-fourth of one per cent. on the value thereof; horses and mules brought to market

Marginal notes:

Tax on retailers, merchants &c.

Amended by act Feb. 25, 1860.

Livery stable, Lotteries, &c.

for sale by other persons than the proprietors of livery stables, one dollar for each ; pistol galleries, fifty dollars; gold watches, fifty cents; silver watches and clocks, thirty-five cents ; gold safety or watch chains, thirty-five cents ; companies for the manufacture of gas, one hundred dollars ; independent of the value of their property : steamboats lying at the wharf for each day or any part thereof, five dollars.

SECTION 7.—*And be it further enacted*, That retailers of spirituous liquors who may procure a license from said City Council of Montgomery, shall be exonerated from paying anything to the county of Montgomery for the privilege of retailing in the city aforesaid.

Retailers to procure license.

Retailers pay no county tax.

SECTION 8.—*And be it further enacted*, That the said Mayor and Aldermen shall be ex-officio, vested with and may exercise in said city, all the powers and authority that belong to Justices of the Peace, by the laws of this State, and the said Marshal shall be ex-officio, Constable, and shall be vested with and exercise all the powers and authority of other Constables of this State ; and the said Mayor, Aldermen and Marshals, shall respectively be liable to the same penalties and restrictions as are imposed by the laws of this State, upon the several offices with which they are invested ; and the Sheriff of said county of Montgomery, and all ministerial officers shall obey the said Mayor and Aldermen, and truly and faithfully execute the warrants and processes committed to them for service, according to the mandate ; and it is made the duty of the Jailor of said county to receive all prisoners committed by warrants of the said Mayor and Aldermen, and the person or persons so committed, safe-

To exercise powers as justices of the peace.

Marshal a Constable.

All officers shall obey the Mayor and Aldermen.

Jailor shall receive prisoners.

ly to keep confined in close Jail till delivered therefrom by due course of law; and the said City Council are hereby authorized to hold their meetings and to keep their records and papers in any room in the Court House of said county, not at the time occupied by the county or any of the county officers.

SECTION 9.—*And be it further enacted,* That should the election not take place on the day fixed for the annual election of Mayor and Aldermen, the corporation shall not for that cause be dissolved, but the incumbents shall remain in office until their successors shall be elected and qualified; and it shall be the duty of the Mayor and Aldermen to fix some day as early as convenient within one month thereafter, on which day the said election shall be held.

SECTION 10.—*And be it further enacted,* That the said inhabitants of the said city shall be exempted
from working on roads and highways out of said city, and from patrol duty, except under the authority of said city, but the streets and highways in said city shall be kept in repair by said city; and the City Council of said city shall have authority
to alter, widen, or extend any street within the limits of the city, whenever in their judgment the
public convenience requires it. When any alteration of a street is determined on by resolution of the City Council, the Mayor of the city shall en-
deavor to acquire the right to the use of the lands necessary for the purpose of alteration by purchase or gift from the proprietor or proprietors. When the Mayor cannot obtain the lands by purchase or otherwise, or when the proprietor or proprietors of any of the lands necessary for the proposed alterations of the streets shall be an infant, *non compos mentis,* non-resident, or person unknown, then the

Mayor shall apply to the Clerk of the Circuit Court for a writ of *ad quod damnum,* to be directed to the Sheriff of Montgomery county, commanding him to summons a jury of seven freeholders of the county, not resident in the city of Montgomery to appear before the Sheriff, on a day named not less than ten days from the date of the writ, and to proceed under his direction, after being sworn impartially to discharge their duty, to assess the value of the lands of such proprietor named in the application for the writ, and in the writ, which shall state the lands required for use as part of the street, and the names of the owners respectively, and the said jury shall, after viewing the premises, render a verdict which may be done by a majority ; which verdict shall be endorsed on the writ by them, and shall assess the damages to each proprietor severally, and the Sheriff shall thereupon return the writ so endorsed to the Clerk of the Circuit Court, and the verdict so rendered shall be entered on the records of the Circuit Court at the next term of the Court after its return, unless an appeal shall have been taken in the manner prescribed in the next section. On the return of the verdict, and the payment to the Clerk of the damages assessed the land so assessed shall enure to the public use as part of the streets unless the City Council, or some proprietor or propritors shall within thirty days take an appeal to the Circuit Court, and on such an appeal being taken the matter shall be tried in the Circuit Court *de novo.* On the suing out of the writ the Mayor shall pay to the Clerk of the Circuit Court two dollars for his fees ; two dollars for each juror, and four dollars for the Sheriff.

Duty of the Sheriff.

Value of land assessed by a jury.

Verdict of Jury to be recorded.

An appeal may be taken.

The Mayor must pay fees, &c.

And all male citizens over eighteen and under forty-five years of age shall be liable to patrol duty, and to serve as guard or watch at such times, and

Citizens liable to perform patrol duty.

in such manner as may be prescribed by the said City Council.

SECTION 11.—*And be it further enacted,* That all

Property vested.

property, claims and demands of whatsoever description belonging to the town of Montgomery, shall be vested in the city of Montgomery, and all debts, contracts and liabilities owning or incurred by said town shall be good and enforced against

said city ; and the corporation of said town shall and may subsist as long as necessary for enforcing and collecting all claims and dues, or the same may be enforced and collected by said city.

SECTION 12.—*And be it further enacted,* That it

Mayor's duty &c.

shall be the duty of the Mayor to preside and keep order at all meeting of the Mayor and Aldermen ; he shall call meetings of the Aldermen whenever in his opinion the interest of the said city may require it ; he shall keep an office in said city and hear and determine upon all causes for breach of the ordinances and by-laws, and shall receive such fees and salary as may be prescribed by the City Council ; in the absence or inability of the Mayor,

Mayor pro tempore.

the Aldermen shall appoint one of their own number Mayor *pro tempore,* who shall discharge the duties of Mayor till the Mayor returns or his inability is removed. Each of the Aldermen may also

Aldermen may hear and determine cases.

hear and determine causes for breach of the by-laws and ordinances ; two Aldermen may call a

Quorum for doing business.

meeting ; the Mayor and three Aldermen, or four Aldermen, shall form a quorum.

SECTION 13.—*And be it further enacted,* That the said City Council may cause an assessment of taxes to be made in each and every year by some proper and fit person or persons ; the assessment naming

Assessment of taxes.

the person liable to such taxes when known, and specifying the property when the owner is not

known, which assessment shall be returned to the
Mayor to be laid before the Mayor and Aldermen,
and the Mayor shall cause at least ten days public
notice that assessment has been made, and the time
when the Mayor and Aldermen will proceed to hear
and determine upon all complaints which may be
made against such assessment, and it shall be their
duty to correct errors and supply omissions; and
when the same has been passed upon by said City
Council, the said assessment shall have the force
and effect of a judgment and execution, and may
be collected by levy and sale of property, on giving
such notice as is required by law on executions from
the Circuit Court, and where no property to be found
is returned upon said assessment, the Mayor may
issue a capias ad satisfaciendum; and all sales of
property made under or by virtue of such assessment shall convey to the purchaser the same title
as if sold by execution from the Circuit Court; and
the collector of said city shall, in case of sale of
real estate, give the purchaser a deed of conveyance,
which shall vest in the purchaser the same interest
that the person had against whom such tax was assessed at the time of such assessment, and where
the owner is not known, the entire equitable and
legal interest in such real estate discharged of all
liens: *Provided,* That where a tax is assessed upon
property, the owners of which are not known,
ninety days' notice of the sale, specifying the property and the tax, shall be given in some newspaper
printed in said city:

And provided, That the duties required of the
said Mayor and Aldermen, except giving notice and
issuing capias ad satisfaciendum, may be devolved
upon a board of assessors, and the assessments ap-

Margin notes:
Mayor shall cause ten days notice to be given.

Correct errors and supply omissions in taxes.

Mayor may issue capias ad satisfaciendum.

Interest of estate sold for taxes.

proved by them shall have the same force and effect as if approved by the Mayor and Aldermen.

Amended by act Feb. 25, 1860.

SECTION 14.—*And be it further enacted*, That the said City Council is hereby authorised and empow-

The city shall have authority to sell real estate for taxes. Owner may redeem.

ered to pass laws for the sale of the real estate in said city for taxes, whether the said real estate belongs to resident or non-resident, owners or to persons unknown, and to authorize the sale of any one lot or subdivision of lot, if seperately assessed, and that the owner or any one for him be allowed to redeem at any time within two years from the sale on paying to the purchaser or the City Treasurer for him four times the amount of the taxes, costs and expenses paid by the purchaser, and interest at the rate of 20 per cent. per annum on the surplus, and that surplus over and above the amount of the taxes, interest, costs and expenses, be paid into the

Treasurers duty.

city Treasury, to be kept by the Treasurer for the owner, upon the responsibility of his bond, and that interest shall be collected, and the taxes assessed from the first day of December next after the assessment, if not paid by that day, and that where any lot or part of a lot has been assessed to an unknown owner, the assessment shall be *prima facie*

City Council may purchase real estate sold for taxes.

evidence of the fact; and that the City Council may, by its agent, purchase real estate sold for taxes; the deed for the same may be made to the Mayor of said city, to be held by him for said city, which may be redeemed as other lands sold for taxes

Duty of Mayor.

as aforesaid, and when redeemed the Mayor shall re-convey to the owner.

SECTION 15.—*And be it further enacted*, That the said "City Council of Montgomery" shall have full

To ordain laws not contrary to constitution and laws of this State.

power and authority to make, ordain and enact such laws and regulations (not contrary to the constitution and laws of this State) as may be deemed necessary in relation to the streets and highways, public buildings and powder magazine, and every other matter and thing which they may deem necessary for the good order and welfare of said city.

SECTION 16.—*And be it further enacted,* That all laws and parts of laws that may contravene this act be and the same are hereby repealed, except so much of any law heretofore passed as may be necessary to carry out and complete any contract with or act of the said town Council of Montgomery, as, may now be incomplete or unsettled.

Repealing clause.

AN ACT

To Amend the Charter of the City of Montgomery.

SECTION 1.—*Be it enacted by the Senate and House of Representatives of the State of Alabama, in General Assembly convened—*

That the City Council of Montgomery be and the same is hereby authorized to raise a sum of money not exceeding seventy-five thousand dollars by the sale of the bonds of said city for that amount, in sums of one hundred dollars each, or upwards, bearing such a rate of interest and redeemable at such times and places as said corporation may designate.

Corporation authorized to sell bonds

SECTION 2.—*And be it further enacted,* That the said corporation be and the same is hereby authorized to pledge or mortgage the real estate belonging to the said corporation, and the rents and profits thereof, for the payment of the principal and interest of said bonds, and to assess such a tax upon the real estate within the corporate limits of said city of Montgomery as shall be fully adequate to the payment of the interest and for a sinking fund for the payment of the principal of said debt.

Property of corporation to be pledged for payment.

SECTION 3.—*And be it further enacted*, That the holders of said bonds shall not be required to inquire into the use or application of the sums of money that shall be raised by the sale of, or advanced upon, said bonds, but that said holders shall be entitled against said corporation to all the advantages of the holders of foreign bills of exchange.

Privileges of bond holders. •

APPROVED February 2, 1846.

. AN ACT

To Repeal An Act imposing restrictions on the City Council of the city of Montgomery, and for other purposes.

SECTION 1.—*Be it enacted by the Senate and House of Representatives of the State of Alabama, in General Assembly convened*—

Repeal.

That An Act imposing restrictions upon the City Council of the city of Mongomery, approved on the third of January, A. D. eighteen hundred and forty-five, be and is hereby repeal.

SECTION 2.—*And be it further enacted*, That the ·City Council of Montgomery shall, from and after the passage of this Act, have full power to collect, demand and receive of and from the owners or consignees of all goods which shall be landed on or shipped from the Montgomery city wharf or wharfs, landing or landings, such wharfage as said Council shall, frm time to time, deem necessary and proper, not exceeding the following rates, to-wit: For each bale of cotton, eight cents; for each barrel five cents; for each sack of coffee, salt, or grain, three cents; for each hogshead or pipe, twenty

Rates wharfage at city wharfs.

cents; for each hundred weight of iron, or other metal, two and a half cents; for all boxes, packages, and merchandise, by measurement, one cent per square foot; for each buggy or sulky, seventy-five cents; for each carriage, one dollar; for each thousand feet of lumber, fifty cents; for each horse or cow, ten cents; for each sheep or hog, two and a half cents; for all steamboats, not exceeding two dollars per day, and all barges or flat boats, one dollar per day they shall remain at said wharfs or landings.

SECTION 3.—*And be it further enacted,* That the said city wharfs or landings shall be located by said City Council on any lands belonging to said City Council on the Eastern bank of the Alabama river, within the corporate limits of said city, public grounds or streets on said bank. *Location of wharves.*

SECTION 4.—*And be it further enacted,* That Fleming Freeman, his executors or assigns, shall have full power to collect, demand and receive of and from owners and consignees of goods and merchandise which shall be landed or shipped from lots numbered one, two and three, in square thirty-five, on Lafayette street, and lot numbered nine, on Fulton street, the same rates of wharfage that are allowed by the second section of this act, or that may be assessed by the City Council, and by them received on the city wharf aforesaid; Provided, that said Fleming Freeman be the *bona fide* owner of the aforesaid lots. *Powers, &c. extended.*

SECTION 5.—*And be it further enacted,* That Charles T. Pollard, and his associates, owners of the Montgomery and West Point Railroad depot wharf, in the city of Montgomery, be and they are hereby entitled to the immunities and privileges of the preceding section of this act.

SECTION 6.—*And be it further enacted,* That nothing in this act shall be construed as to prejudice the *Construction of act.*

3

rights of Francis M. Gilmer, Jr., and his associates, contained in the act to incorporate the Planters' wharf and steamboat company, in the town of Montgomery, approved January the sixteenth, eighteen hundred and thirty-two.

SECTION 7.—*And be it further enacted,* That all laws in any way contravening this act, or any part thereof, are hereby repealed.

APPROVED 13th January, 1846.

AN ACT

To Amend an Act Incorporating the City of Montgomery, Approved 22d December, 1837.

SECTION 1.—*Be it enacted by the Senate and House of Representatives of the State of Alabama, in General Assembly convened—*

That the City Council of Montgomery be, and is hereby empowered, in addition to the powers already conferred by said act, to pass ordinances or by-laws to regulate the erection of wooden buildings in such parts of said city as in the opinion of the Council the public good may require, and pass ordinances for the punishment of such as may injure or deface the public buildings or grounds.

Certain powers may be exercised.

APPROVED, February 26, 1848.

AN ACT

To authorize Appeals from the Decisions of the Mayor and Aldermen of the city of Montgomery.

SECTION 1.—*Be it enacted by the Senate and House of Representatives of the State of Alabama, in General Assembly convened—*

That from and after the passage of this Act, an appeal may be had to the Circuit Court of Montgomery county, upon all judgments rendered by the Mayor and Aldermen of the city of Montgomery, in like manner and upon the same terms and conditions as now prescribed by law in cases of appeal from decisions of Justices of the Peace.

APPROVED February 10th, 1852.

AN ACT

To amend the City Charter of Montgomery, and for other purposes.

SECTION 1.—*Be it enacted by the Senate and House of Representatives of the State of Alabama, in General Assembly convened—*

That authority is given to the city of Montgomery to subscribe for five thousand shares of the capital stock of the Alabama and Florida Railroad Company, and to issue its bonds, and deliver the same to said Company, according to the provisions of an ordinance of said city, passed by its corporate authorities on the 20th day of June, 1853; and the authority to pass such ordinances is hereby legalized and confirmed.

SECTION 2.—*And be it further enacted,* That the

conditions and limitations imposed by said ordinance upon such subscription may be changed, altered, or abrogated by the corporate authorities of said city, with the consent of the Alabama and Florida Railroad Company; and authority is hereby given to the corporate authorities of said city to pledge any property, or the rents and profits of the same, belonging to said city, to the payment of its bonds issued in payment of said stock, or to levy a special tax on the real estate within the corporate limits of said city to any amount the corporate authorities may think proper, to pay the interest on said bonds.

APPROVED February 15, 1854.

————•————

AN ACT

To Amend the Charter of the City of Montgomery.

SECTION 1.—*Be it enacted by the Senate and House of Representatives of the State of Alabama, in General Assembly convened—*

The State House debt.

That the City Council of Montgomery be, and the same is hereby authorized to extend the unpaid portion of the debt known as the State House debt, created under authority of an Act of the Legislature, approved February 2nd, 1846, either by a renewal of the bonds in the hands of the present holders, or by the sale of new bonds, in lieu of the old; said renewed debt to be payable in not less than eight nor more than twelve years from the maturity of the present outstanding bonds, to bear not exceeding eight per cent. interest, and to be negotiated at rate not less than par, and in the event of the sale of new bonds, the proceeds thereof shall be applied to the payment of such outstanding bonds, and no other purpose whatever.

SECTION 2.—*And be it further enacted*, That the income accruing from the wharves of said city shall be devoted and exclusively applied to the payment of the actual debt of the city hitherto incurred, and interest thereon, and in addition thereto, the said City Council shall have power to levy and collect an annual tax, not exceeding one-fourth of one per cent., on the value of the real estate of said city, which said tax and wharf income shall be paid to the city Treasurer, to be by him applied to the liquidation of said actual city debt hitherto incurred, and interest thereon, and no other purpose whatsoever until the same is fully paid.

SECTION 3.—*And be it further enacted*, That for the ordinary current expenses of said city, the said City Council may levy and collect a tax on real estate not exceeding one-half of one per cent. on the cash value thereon, and no more in any one year, and it shall not be lawful for the said City Council of Montgomery to contract any debt, or incur any liability for, on account of said city of Montgomery, which is not to be paid out of the ordinary current revenue of the year in which said debt or liability is contracted or incurred, and any such debt or liability attempted to be contracted or incurred by said City Council in violation of the foregoing provisions shall be void as against said city of Montgomery.

APPROVED February 15, 1856.

THE CODE

OF THE

CITY OF MONTGOMERY:

MEMBERS OF THE CORPORATION IN 1861.

ANDREW J. NOBLE, Mayor.

ALDERMEN:

Ward No. 1.
GEORGE M. FIGH,
E. A. JANNEY.

Ward No. 4.
JOHN P. DICKERSON,
THOMAS O. GLASCOCK.

Ward No. 2.
WALTER C. JACKSON,
A. HOWARD.

Ward No. 5.
MARION A. CHISHOLM,
WM. A. OGBOURNE.

Ward No. 3.
HUGH W. WATSON,
WM. C. C. FOSTER.

Ward No. 6.
JOHN FRASER,
GEORGE R. SAYRE.

OFFICERS OF THE CITY FOR 1861.

City Clerk—AUGUSTUS UNDERWOOD.
City Treasurer—SAMUEL LACY.
Chief Eng. of the Fire Depart.—JAMES P. STOW.
First Asst. Eng. of the Fire Dep.—ALEX. R. BELL.
Second Asst. Eng. of the Fire Dep.—JNO. B. GARRETT.
Third Asst. Eng. of the Fire Dep.—FORT HARGROVE.
Wharfinger—RICHARD FRASIER.
Clerk of the Magazine—FRANCIS MONFEE.
Clerk of the Market—HUGH McLEAN.
Marshal—ISAAC G. MAXWELL.
Deputy Marshal—W. W. BALL.
Captain of Police—THOMAS REED.
Sexton—NOAH GREGORY.

4

THE CODE

OF THE

CITY OF MONTGOMERY:

CHAPTER I.

GENERAL PROVISIONS APPLICABLE TO THIS CODE.

§ 1.—Words used in this Code, in the past or present tense, include the future as well as the past and present. Words used in the masculine gender include the feminine and neuter; the singular includes the plural, and the plural the singular. *Words used in this Code*

§ 2.—The word "property" includes property real and personal. The words "real property" are co-extensive with lands, tenements, and hereditaments. The words "personal property" include money, goods, chattels, things in action and evidences of debt, deeds and conveyances. *Property includes both real and personal property.*

§ 3.—The term "negro" includes mulatto, and all persons of mixed blood, descended on the part of the father or mother from negro ancestors to the third generation inclusive, though one ancestor of each generation may have been a white person. *The term "negro" includes persons of mixed blood, descended from negro ancestors.*

CHAPTER II.

AFFRAYS, ASSAULT AND BATTERY, ARRESTS, AND APPEALS.

Any person guilty of an affray shall be fined.

§ 4.—Every person who shall be guilty of an affray in which neither a stick nor a weapon is used, shall be fined five dollars ; and in default of payment thereof, shall be imprisoned not exceeding twenty days.

Any person committing an affray and using a stick, shall be fined.

§ 5.—Any person committing an affray, and using a stick, or other weapon, shall be fined twenty dollars, and on failing to pay the fine, may be imprisoned not exceeding thirty days.

Any person using fire-arms, or other deadly weapons shall be fined.

§ 6.—Every person using fire-arms, or other deadly weapon in an affray, shall be fined fifty dollars, and on failing to pay the fine, shall be imprisoned not exceeding sixty days.

Any person committing an assault and battery.

§ 7.—Any person who shall commit an assault and battery upon a white person, shall be fined not less than five nor more than twenty-five dollars.

An assault with a stick or weapon not likely to cause death

§ 8.—Any person who shall commit an assault and battery upon a white person with a stick, or any weapon not likely to cause death, shall be fined not less than twenty, nor more than fifty dollars.

An assault with fire-arms or deadly weapons.

§ 9.—Every person who shall commit an assault with firearms, or other deadly weapons, shall be fined fifty dollars.

An assault and battery upon a slave.

§ 10.—Any person who shall commit an assault and battery upon a slave, within the limits of the city, shall, upon the complaint of the master, his agent, or any one controlling such slave, be fined not more than ten dollars.

An assault upon a slave with deadly weapons.

§ 11.—Any person who shall commit an assault upon a slave, with a deadly weapon, shall be fined not less than twenty, nor more than fifty dollars.

§ 12. A slave, who shall commit an assault or an assault and battery upon a white person, shall be punished by any number of stripes not exceeding one hundred.

§ 13.—A slave, who shall commit an assault and battery on a slave or free negro, shall upon conviction before the Mayor or an Alderman, receive not exceeding fifty stripes.

§ 14.—Any free negro, who shall commit an assault and battery upon a slave, shall be fined ten dollars, or be punished by any number of stripes, not exceeding fifty, according to the discretion of the Mayor or Alderman, before whom the case may be tried.

§ 15.—Any free negro, committing an assault and battery upon a free negro, shall be fined ten dollars, and if the assault be made with a deadly weapon, such free negro shall be fined not less than twenty, nor more than fifty dollars, and in default of the payment thereof, shall receive not exceeding one hundred stripes.

§ 16.—Any free negro, committing an assault and battery upon a white person shall be punished by any number of stripes not exceeding one hundred.

§ 17.—On the trial of a person for an assault and battery, or an affray, he or she may prove any opprobrious language or abusive epithets, used by the person assaulted or beaten, at or near the time of the assault and battery or affray, in justification of his or her conduct; and the proof of abusive language being uttered, may or may not be a defence to the charge, according to the judgment of the Mayor or Alderman by whom the case may be tried.

§ 18.—Any person arrested by the Marshal or policeman for the violation of an ordinance of the city, shall be taken forthwith before the Mayor or an Alderman for trial, unless the arrest be made at a time when a trial cannot be had. In such a case the officer shall allow the person arrested a reasonable time to give a bond with sufficient sureties for not less than one hundred, nor more than two hundred dollars, conditioned for his or her appearance before the Mayor at a specified time, and for the payment of all fines and costs, which may be imposed.

ken before the Mayor for trial.

May give bond conditioned to appear before the Mayor at a specified time.

§ 19.—Any person, arrested for a violation of an ordinance of the city, who shall fail to give the bond above described, shall be imprisoned in the guard-house until he or she can be brought before the Mayor or an Alderman for trial.

A person failing to give bond shall be imprisoned until a trial can be had.

§ 20.—Any person fined or imprisoned by the Mayor or an Alderman, may appeal to the City Council, but such person if required by the Mayor or Alderman shall give a bond with sureties for twice the amount of fine and costs, conditioned to pay the fine and costs, which may be imposed according to the ordinances of the city.

An appeal may be taken from the decision of the Mayor or an Alderman to the City Council.

CHAPTER III.

ANIMALS RUNNING AT LARGE IN THE CITY—HORSES, MULES, CATTLE, HOGS AND DOGS.

§ 21.—All cattle, running at large within the fire limits of the city, between the fifteenth day of October, and the fifteenth day of March, shall be seized and sold.

All animals running at large shall be seized.

§ 22.—The Marshal shall take up and confine all cattle so running at large in the city, and shall

The Marshal take up cattle running at

advertise them forthwith at the door of the Court-House, at the Post-Office, and at the Market-House, for ten successive days; such advertisement shall fully describe the brand, mark, and general appearance of the cattle, and shall state the time and place of sale. If the cattle advertised, are not claimed before the expiration of ten days, or at the time of sale, the Marshal shall sell them singly to the highest bidder, for cash, and account to the City Council for the money.

large, and advertise them for sale, &c.

§ 23.—Every officer of the city, who shall bid or be directly or indirecty interested in any purchase, made at such sale, shall be fined on conviction before the Mayor or any Alderman in the sum of twenty-five dollars.

No officer of the city sh'll bid at such sale,

§ 24.—The owner or the owner's agent, who may claim the cattle, taken up under this ordinance, upon the payment of fifty cents upon each head for the use of the city, and twenty-five cents for each head, for every day they were fed by the city, shall receive the cattle from the City Marshal.

The owner of the cattle may receive them upon paying fifty cents.

§ 25.—The refusal or failure of the Marshal to deliver the cattle upon the compliance of the owner or his agent, with this ordinance, shall be punished by a fine of not less than ten nor more than fifty dollars.

The Marshal refusing to deliver the cattle shall be punished.

§ 26. No owner of hogs, shall permit them to run at large within the limits of the city, under the penalty of having them seized and sold.

Hogs shall not run at large in the city.

§ 27.—The Marshal shall take up and confine hogs, running at large, and forthwith advertise them at the Post-Office, and at the Market-House, for six successive days, describing the marks and appearance of the hogs, and mentioning the time

*The Marshal shall take up hogs running at large and advertise them.
If any person claim*

and place of sale, and if no person shall claim the hogs, the Marshal shall sell them in suitable lots to the highest bidder for cash, and account to the City Council for the money.

them they shall be sold to the highest bidder for cash.

§ 28.—Any officer of the city, who shall bid or be directly or indirectly interested in any purchase made at such sale, shall be fined, on conviction before the Mayor or an Alderman in the sum of twenty-five dollars.

Any officer bidding, or being interested in the purchase of hogs shall be fined.

§ 29.—The Marshal, upon the payment by the owner or his agent of one dollar for each hog claimed, shall deliver the hog or hogs to the owner or his agent, and shall pay the money so collected to the City Treasurer.

The Marshal shall deliver the hogs to the owner or his agent.

§ 30.—The Marshal shall take up and confine in a livery stable, any horse or mule, running at large in the city, and immediately post an advertisement at the door of the Court-House, Post-Office and Market, containing a discription of the animal and stating the time and place of sale, and shall notify the owner if known.

The Marshal shall take up a horse or mule running at large.

§ 31.—The Marshal, after giving notice for ten successive days as aforesaid, shall sell the horse or mule at the time and place appointed to the highest bidder for cash.

After a notice of ten days the horse or mule shall be sold.

§ 32.—Any person claiming such property before or at the time of sale, upon proof of ownership, and the payment of one dollar to the City Treasurer, and all reasonable charges for the support of the animal, shall receive it from the Marshal.

Any person proving ownership of horse or mule shall receive it.

§ 33.—Any owner, who shall prove his title to any horse or mule within one year from the sale thereof, shall receive from the City Treasury, the amount of money paid in as the proceeds of such sale.

The owner proving title to any horse or mule sold by the Marshal, shall receive proceeds of sale.

§ 34.—The City Marshal shall procure neat and cheap dog collars, which he shall sell to any white person, applying to him for such a collar at the price which was paid for it, and the Marshal shall mark the number of the collar upon it, and register the name of the purchaser, for which he shall be paid ten cents.

§ 35.—Nothing in the preceding section shall be so construed as to prevent the owner of a dog obtaining a collar elsewhere, which shall be numbered, and the name of the owner registered by the Marshal in the usual way, upon the receipt of ten cents.

§ 36.—The Marshal shall kill every dog without a collar regularly numbered, which may be running in the streets, unless it be under the management or control of some person at the time.

§ 37.—The Marshal shall not sell, give, nor in any manner dispose of a dog collar to a slave or free negro, and any white person purchasing a collar for, or giving, selling, or bartering a collar to a slave or free negro, shall be fined ten dollars.

§ 38.—Every slave who shall keep a dog in the city, shall receive any number of stripes not exceeding thirty-nine, unless the owner of the slave will pay a fine of five dollars.

§ 39.—Every free negro who shall keep a dog on his or her premises, or under his or her control in the city, without a license from the Mayor, shall be fined five dollars.

CHAPTER IV.

ARTESIAN WELLS AND BASIN—BATHING IN ARTESIAN BASIN OR RIVER.

No person shall wash any vehicle or animal near the artesian wells

§ 41.—Every person who shall wash a buggy, carriage, omnibus, or other vehicle, or wash any animal in the streets of the city within fifty feet of the artesian wells, shall be fined five dollars.

No person shall throw anything in the artesion basin, &c.

§ 42.—Every person who shall throw anything into the artesian basin, in court square, or injure the artesian wells in any manner, shall be fined five dollars for the first offence, and ten dollars for every subsequent offence.

No person must bathe in the basin or in the river within certain limits.

§ 43.—Every person who shall bathe in the artesian basin at any time, or in the river within two hundred yards of the wharves or ferries in the limits of the city, between sunrise and dark, shall be fined not more than five dollars.

Slaves violating sections of this chapter punished.

§ 44.—Every slave who shall violate any section of this chapter shall receive not exceeding thirty-nine stripes, unless his or her master or employer will pay a fine of five dollars.

Free negro violating the foregoing section fined or imprisoned.

§ 45.—Any free negro who shall violate the foregoing sections shall receive not exceeding fifty lashes, or be fined not more than ten dollars, according to the discretion of the Mayor or Aldermen, before whom the accused may be carried.

CHAPTER V.

BARBERS.

Barbers shall not keep open after eleven o'clock.

§ 46.—Any person keeping open a Barber shop on the Sabbath, after eleven o'clock, A. M., shall be fined ten dollars.

CHAPTER VI.

BURGLARY AND LARCENY.

§ 47.—Every person who shall be convicted of burglary or larceny shall be fined not less than five nor more fifty dollars.

Person committing burglary or larceny shall be fined.

§ 48.—Every slave, or free negro, who shall commit burglary or larceny, shall receive not exceeding fifty lashes on the bare back.

Slaves or free negroes guilty of burglary or larceny, &c.

§ 49.—Any person who shall buy, receive, or conceal chattels or merchandise, knowing that the same had been stolen, shall be fined not less than five nor more than fifty dollars ; and any slave or free negro violating this section, shall receive not exceeding fifty stripes.

Persons concealing or buying stolen goods shall be fined.

§ 50.—Every person who shall obtain money or goods under false pretences, or practise a fraud upon another, shall be fined not less than five nor more than fifty dollars.

A person obtaining goods or money under false pretence fined.

———

CHAPTER VII.

CABS, CARRIAGES, HACKS AND OMNIBUSES, CARTS, DRAYS AND WAGONS.

§ 51.—The owner of a cab, carriage, or hack, kept for hire, shall pay, annually, twenty-five dollars for a license for each vehicle ; any person failing to do so, shall be fined ten dollars, and five dollars thereafter for every day this section shall be violated.

The owner of any cab or hack must procure license.

Penalty.

§ 52.—No license shall be issued to any person to run a carriage, hack, dray, wagon, or other vehicle for hire, unless the applicant shall make and subscribe an oath that the vehicle for which a

The applicant for a license shall make oath that it is for his exclusive benefit.

license is desired, shall be used for his sole and exclusive benefit, so long as the license remains in his name, and if transferred by order of the City Council to another person, the transferree shall make and subscribe to the same oath.

The Clerk must register license. No license transferable without consent of the Council.

§ 53.—The Clerk of the city shall register the name of the owner of a licensed vehicle, the place of his residence, and the number of the license; and no license shall be transferred without the consent of the City Council; and any person violating this section shall be fined not less than five nor more than twenty dollars.

Penalty.

The lamps of all public vehicles must have the number of the vehicle painted on them, and must be lighted from dark till morning

§ 54.—The owner of a public vehicle, shall have its number painted on its lamps, in figures not less than three inches long, so as to be easily seen, and while on the streets, the lamps of such vehicles must be lighted from dusk until morning; and any person failing to do so, shall be fined ten dollars, and five dollars for each day thereafter the owner shall violate this section.

The rates which hackmen may be allowed to charge.

§ 55.—Hackmen shall not charge for their services more than the following rates, viz: For carrying a passenger to any place within the city, twenty-five cents; for a passenger with baggage, not exceeding one hundred pounds in weight, fifty cents, and for each additional package, ten cents. After ten o'clock at night, the rates above mentioned may be doubled, except against passengers to and from railroad depots, and steamboat landings.

One dollar an hour for the use of the vehicle may be charged.

§ 56.—The owner or driver of a licensed vehicle, notwithstanding the rates above mentioned, may, upon agreement, charge the person one dollar an hour for the use of the whole vehicle.

Persons refusing to pay the driver

§ 57.—Any person refusing to pay the owner or driver the foregoing rates for services rendered, shall be fined not less than two nor more than five dollars.

§ 58.—Any white driver, who shall charge more than the established rates shall be fined ten dollars, to be collected from the driver, owner, or agent of the vehicle; and any slave or free negro, who shall charge more than the foregoing rates shall receive not exceeding thirty-nine lashes in addition to the fine imposed.

ver shall be fined.

A white driver charging more than above rates to be fined, and a negro driver flogged.

§ 59.—Any owner, agent, or driver of a licensed vehicle, who shall refuse to carry persons according to the provisions of this ordinance shall be fined not less than five, nor more than fifteen dollars, and if the driver be a slave or free negro, he shall receive not exceeding thirty-nine stripes, in addition to the fine imposed on such owner or agent.

Any driver refusing to carry passengers, fined, if a negro driver, he shall be flogged.

§ 60.—Every person who shall hire a horse or vehicle of any kind to a slave or free negro without a written permission from the owner, or overseer of the slave, or from the guardian of the free negro, or shall permit such slave or free negro to ride in any vehicle shall be fined ten dollars; and if the driver of the licensed vehicle so hired or used, be a slave or free negro, he shall receive not more than thirty-nine stripes in addition to the fine imposed on the owner or agent of the vehicle.

Any person hiring a horse or vehicle to a slave without permission shall be fined.

§ 61.—The owner or driver of a licensed vehicle, who shall keep it on the streets in front of a dwelling or store, against the consent of the owner or occupant thereof, shall be fined not less than five, nor more than twenty dollars, and if the driver be a slave or free negro he shall receive not exceeding thirty-nine stripes.

No driver shall keep his vehicle on the street in front of a house aga'st the consent of the occupant.

§ 62.—Every driver of a licensed vehicle, who shall quarrel or be guilty of noisy and disorderly

Any driver guilty of disorderly con-

conduct; or who shall drive against or interfere with other vehicles or animals, shall be fined not less than five, nor more than twenty dollars; and if such driver be a slave or free negro, he shall also receive not more than thirty-nine lashes.

§ 63.—Every driver of a public vehicle, who shall block up a street or thoroughfare, or who shall leave the seat of his vehicle, or be distant from his horses heads more than ten feet unless engaged in receiving or delivering baggage, for which purpose he may go a reasonable distance, and be gone a reasonable length of time, shall be fined not less than five, nor more than twenty dollars, and if he be a slave or free negro, he shall receive not exceeding thirty-nine lashes, in addition to the fine imposed on the owner or agent.

§ 64.—Every owner or driver of a licensed vehicle, who shall race or drive at a speed dangerous to persons on the streets, shall be fined not less than ten, nor more than fifty dollars, and if the driver be a slave or free negro, he shall receive not exceeding thirty-nine stripes in addition to the fine imposed on the owner or agent.

§ 65.—Every driver of a public vehicle, who, meeting other vehicles of any kind, shall neglect to drive on the right side of the street or thoroughfare, (if it be possible to do so,) shall be fined five dollars, and any slave or free negro violating this section shall receive not more than twenty lashes.

§ 66.—Every driver of a public vehicle, who shall fail to stop instantly when hailed by the Marshal or a policeman, shall be fined five dollars, and if he be a slave or free negro he shall receive not exceeding thirty-nine stripes.

§ 67.—Every owner or driver of a public vehicle, who shall neglect to have the sections of this Code

---

Marginal notes:

duct, or driving agai'st other vehicles punished.

The drivers of licensed vehicles shall not obstruct the street, nor leave their horses, &c.

Drivers shall not run nor drive at a speed dangerous to the lives of the citizens.

Drivers of public vehicles meeting others must drive to the right, &c.

All drivers upon being hailed by a policeman must stop instantly.

Sections numbered must be

numbered fifty-five, fifty-six, fifty-seven, fifty-eight, and fifty-nine, hung up in some conspicuous place inside his vehicle at all times when in use, shall be fined ten dollars.

printed and hung up in the vehicle.

§ 68.—The owner of a public omnibus, shall pay one hundred dollars for a license for each omnibus, drawn by four horses, and fifty dollars for a license for each omnibus, drawn by two horses; and the owners and drivers shall be governed by the same rules, and be subject to the same penalties as the owners and drivers of licensed carriages, cabs, and hacks.

The owner of omnibuses must pay for license and be governed by same rules as licensed hacks, &c.

§ 69.—The City Clerk shall have this chapter of the City Code printed in a pamphlet form, and shall furnish a copy of it to every owner or agent of any licensed vehicle.

this chapter must be printed for owners of vehicles.

§ 70.—Every person who shall run a dray, cart, wagon, or other vehicle of like kind, without obtaining a license, for which twenty dollars shall be paid, if the vehicle be drawn by not more than two animals, or thirty dollars if it be drawn by three, and forty dollars if it be drawn by four animals, shall be fined ten dollars.

Drays, carts, and wagons must be licensed.

§ 71.—The City Clerk, upon receiving the additional sum of twenty cents, shall furnish the applicant with the number of the license granted, stamped or printed on tin, which shall be fastened in a conspicuous place on the vehicle licensed; and any dray, cart, wagon, or vehicle of like kind not having in its number affixed to it, shall be considered "not licensed."

The clerk to stamp the number of license which number to be fastened on vehicle.

§ 72.—The owner of a licensed dray, cart, or wagon who, or his driver, shall refuse without a sufficient excuse, between the hours of sunrise and sunset, to carry a load to any part of the city, shall be fined not more than ten dollars.

Any driver refusing to carry load shall be fined.

§ 73.-- The following articles or their equivalent, shall be considered a full load, viz: five hundred feet of lumber, or one hogshead of sugar, molasses, tobacco, coffee, rice or liquor ; four barrels of liquor or provisions, three barrels of molasses, six sacks of salt or any other article not exceeding twelve hundred pounds ; and any person hauling a load in a licensed vehicle of any kind to any part of the city, who shall charge more than forty cents for such service, shall be fined five dollars.

§ 74.--All licenses, granted to the owners of carts, drays, wagons, or other vehicles, of the kind, shall expire on the first day of March of each year. But the City Clerk may issue such a license at any time, and charge at the rate above stated.

§ 75.—Every white driver of a cart, dray, or wagon, who shall drive faster than a walk, in any of the streets of the city shall be fined five dollars, and any slave or free negro violating this section, shall receive not exceeding thirty-nine lashes.

§ 76.—Every person who shall ride or drive through the streets or public grounds of the city at a gait faster than eight miles and hour, unless he be a physician or going for a physician, shall on conviction before the Mayor or an Alderman, be fined five dollars for the first, and ten dollars for each subsequent offence.

CHAPTER VIII.

CEMETERY AND SEXTON.

§ 77.—Any person who shall bury a corpse within the limits of the city, except in the cemetery, and under the superintendence of the sexton, shall be fined twenty dollars.

(Marginal notes: What articles shall constitute a load. No one shall charge more than forty cents a load. All licenses shall expire on first day of March of each year. Driving carts, buggies, &c., fast, forbidden. Riding or driving any vehicle faster than eight miles an hour. All persons buried in the city must be buried in the grave yard.)

§ 78.—Every person who shall injure or destroy the fence or gates of the grave yard, or the tombs, monuments, or any structure erected to enclose or mark a grave, shall be fined not exceeding fifty dollars.

§ 79.—Every person who shall break, cut, dig up, or destroy a tree, shrub, or flower, upon any lot in the burying ground, unless it be owned by such person, shall be fined not exceeding fifty dollars.

§ 80.—Any slave or free negro, who shall violate either of the preceding sections, shall receive not less than fifty stripes.

§ 81.—Any person who shall enclose a lot in the old part of the grave yard, without the permission of the City Council, or in the new part without having purchased it from the City Council, shall be fined twenty dollars.

§ 82.—The City Council shall annually elect a city Sexton, who shall hold his office for the term of one year.

§ 83.—The Sexton shall keep a map of the burying ground and a book, containing the name of every person interred, the place of nativity, the age, the late residence, and the time of residence in the city, and the cause of the death of the deceased.

§ 84.—The Sexton shall make an alphabetical index to the book, and shall, without charge, exhibit the book and map to any person applying to him, and shall, upon the request of such person, point out any grave in the Cemetery.

§ 85.—The Sexton shall dig, or superintend the digging, of all graves, which must be not less than five feet in depth, and inter all corpses carried to the city grave-yard.

42

The Sexton shall keep the grounds in good order.

§ 86.—The Sexton shall keep the grounds in good order, and the fence in such condition as to exclude all stock; and shall open and close the gates when necessary.

The Sexton must make a monthly report.

§ 87.—The Sexton shall report monthly to the City Council the number of interments made by him.

The Sexton shall receive compensation for superintending a burial.

§ 88.—For superintending the digging of a grave and interment of an adult, the Sexton shall receive three dollars, and for a person under twelve years of age, one half this amount.

A pauper, slave or free negro shall not be buried in the new part of the grave yard, &c.

§ 89.—The Sexton shall not bury a pauper, slave, or free negro, in the new part of the grave yard, except on the margin and extreme North side of the enclosure, and all strangers, not owning lots, shall be interred only on the lots included between the numbers one hundred and forty-four and one hundred and sixty-five.

The Sexton violating the ordinances or neglecting duty shall be fined or dismissed.

§ 90.—The Sexton, neglecting or refusing to perform any duties prescribed, or violating the preceding sections in any manner, shall be fined ten dollars, or dismissed from office, or may be both fined and dismissed, according to the discretion of the City Council.

Upon the resignation or removal of a Sexton he must deliver map, books, &c., to Mayor.

§ 91.—Upon the removal or resignation of the Sexton, or the appointment of his successor, the Sexton shall deliver to the Mayor the map of the burying ground and the books containing the list of interments.

CHAPTER IX.

CHIMNEYS.

Chimneys shall not be burnt at

§ 92.—Every owner or occupant of a house who shall burn its chimneys between the hours of 5 o'clock, P. M., and 9 o'clock, A. M., unless it be raining at the time, shall be fined five dollars for each offence.

night except it be raining

§ 93.—All chimneys, stoves, furnaces, or other fire-places, on any premises liable to burn and endanger the property adjoining, are hereby declared to be nuisances; and the owner or lessee of the premises shall repair or remove such chimney, stove, or furnace, according to the direction of the City Council.

All chimneys, stoves &c., liable to burn and endanger property are nuisances.

§ 94.—Any person neglecting, beyond a reasonable time, to comply with the order of the City Council, shall be fined ten dollars for each day such nuisance may continue.

Any person neglecting to abate the nuisance &c fined.

CHAPTER X.

CITY CLERK.

§ 95.—Before the City Clerk enters upon the duties of his office, he shall make the following oath, or affirmation, viz: "I, ——, will well and truly perform all the duties of Clerk of the City Council of Montgomery, to the best of my skill and ability, so help me God." He shall also give bond, with sureties, for such sum as the City Council may from time to time direct and approve.

The City Clerk must make oath before entering upon discharge of his duty.

§ 96.—The City Clerk shall attend every meeting and keep the minutes of its proceedings; he shall record in a book all transcripts, accounts of officers, instruments of writing, contracts or reports, which may be ordered by the City Council to be recorded; and shall take charge of and preserve the books, papers, and records belonging to the city.

Clerk shall attend meetings of City Council keep minutes records transcripts, &c.

§ 97.—The Clerk shall issue every summons and process which may be required of him, for the just execution of the laws of the city.

§ 98.—The Clerk, under the direction and control of the City Council, shall issue all **warrants** upon the City Treasury, but in no case must he issue such a warrant, unless it be according to an order, made in open Council, by the Mayor and at least six Aldermen, or in the absence of the Mayor, by at least seven Aldermen, nor for any other amount than that contained in the official proceedings, signed by himself and the Mayor. The Clerk shall keep an account of all warrants issued by him, and shall record the date and number of the warrant, and the amount of money for which it was issued, to whom made payable, by whom it was received, and take a receipt from the person to whom it was paid.

§ 99.—The Clerk shall open a set of books, in which he shall enter all appropriations made by the City Council, and keep an account of the expenditures of the city.

§ 100.—At the end of each month, the Clerk shall deliver to the City Treasurer all the money in his possession, and render an account to the City Council, at its first meeting in every month, of the money received and paid by him to the City Treasurer. The account must contain the amount of money, the day on which, and the name of the person from whom, it was received; and also must state the means by which it was obtained, whether by fines, taxes, licenses, or otherwise; and such account, after being examined and approved by the City Council, shall be recorded, and considered to be *prima facie* correct.

The Clerk shall deliver to the City Treasurer the money in his possession.

The Clerk shall render an account to the City Council.

§ 101.—The Clerk shall receive the returns of the taxes of all persons liable to be taxed by the city, and for this purpose he shall attend at his office from two o'clock till five o'clock, P. M., of every day from the first to the twentieth day of March of each year.

The Clerk shall receive returns of taxes.

§ 102.—All persons shall furnish to the Clerk a list of their taxable property in the city, and make the following oath or affirmation, viz: "I, ———— do swear or affirm that the list I have rendered to the Clerk includes all the real and personal property subject to taxation in the city of Montgomery, which I have in my possession in my own right, or have in my possession or control belonging to any other person, so help me God." And in case any person shall refuse to deliver the list aforesaid, the Clerk, according to the best of his information, shall make out a list of the taxable property owned by such person, and the same shall be doubly taxed; but, before doing so, the Clerk must demand the said list of the delinquent, at his or her residence, or leave a notice for him or her to furnish the list within forty-eight hours, and for every such visit the Clerk shall receive from the tax payer twenty cents.

Persons must furnish a list of their taxable property, &c.

§ 103.—The City Clerk shall assess and collect the taxes upon all personal property subject to taxation.

The Clerk shall assess and collect taxes, &c.

§ 104.—The City Clerk, each year, before commencing the assessment, shall prepare an alphabetical list of the voters of the city, who voted at the preceding election, and arrange the names in the Wards in which they voted. As each person whose name is on the list is assessed, he shall note it opposite to the name, and every person whose

The Clerk shall make out a list of the voters of the city.

name is not on the list, shall be added thereto when he is assessed.

§ 105.—The Clerk shall carefully examine the names of the persons assessed at the last assessment of taxes, and add those which do not appear on the list, so that each years' returns of persons assessed, and the list of voters, may aid him in making a full assessment.

The names persons assessed at the last assessment.

§ 106.—The Clerk shall also make an alphabetical digest of the returns of taxable property, containing the real estate of each individual, and lay it before the City Council on or before the twentieth day of April of each year, and the Mayor shall, forthwith, deliver the said schedule to the assessors appointed by the City Council.

Alphabetical digest of the returns of taxable property.

§ 107.—The schedule delivered to the assessors, shall contain the names, when known, of the persons liable to taxation, and, when unknown, it shall state that the property belongs to persons unknown; and after the property mentioned in the schedule shall have been assessed, and the assessment approved by the City Council, the Clerk shall collect the taxes imposed, on or before the first day of December of each year.

What the schedule delivered to the assessors must state.

Clerk must collect the taxes.

§ 108.—The Clerk shall grant the licenses required by the city laws, in every instance in which the applicant shall comply with the conditions imposed by the City Council, and shall, if requested, issue subpœnas for witnesses in all cases tried before the city authorities.

The Clerk shall grant licenses, issue subpœnas, &c.

CHAPTER XI.

DISORDERLY CONDUCT.

§ 109.—Every person, who shall quarrel in a loud tone, or use profane or indecent language in a public place, or in a private place loud enough to be heard by neighbors; or shall act in an indecent, riotous, or disorderly manner in the streets, or at any place in the city, shall be fined ten dollars, and may at the discretion of the Mayor or Alderman trying the case, be compelled to give bond with sureties, in any sum not exceeding five hundred dollars for his or her good behavior for six months.

No person shall quarrel loudly, or use profane or indecent language, or act in a disorderly manner.

Bond for good behaviour.

§ 110.—Any person, who shall injure, break down, destroy, or carry away a fence, gate, step or door of a house, or shall take down, deface, or carry away any sign-board, plate or card which indicates the name, occupation, or business of a person or shall commit any like offence, shall be fined ten dollars.

Persons injuring fences, gates, &c.

§ 111.—Every minor or apprentice, who shall violate either of the two preceding sections, shall be committed to prison for ten days, unless the parent, guardian, master or mistress of such minor or apprentice, will pay a fine of ten dollars and costs.

A minor or apprentice violating preceding sections.

§ 112.—Every person, who shall maliciously kill, cripple, or commit any act of cruelty, on a domestic animal in the city, shall be fined five dollars.

Cruelty to animals.

§ 113.—Every person, who shall engage in cock-fighing, or in making dogs or other animals fight, in the city, shall be fined five dollars for every such offence.

Cock fighting, &c.

§ 114.—Every slave who shall violate either of the two preceding sections shall receive not exceed thirty-nine lashes; and every free negro, who shall violate either of the said sections shall receive not exceeding thirty-nine

A slave or free negro violating preceding sections.

nine stripes, or be fined ten dollars at the discretion of the Mayor or Alderman trying the case.

Drunkenness shall be punished. § 115.—Any person drunk, and lying or staggering about the streets, or on the sidewalks of the city, or other public place, shall on conviction before the Mayor or an Alderman be fined five dollars for every such offence.

All gambling prohibited. § 116.—All persons who shall within the limits of the city play at any game or suffer gaming on their premises contrary to the laws of the State, shall on conviction before the Mayor or an Alderman be fined fifty dollars.

Persons gaming with slave or permitting slaves or free negroes to game on their premises. § 117.—Every person who shall play at any game, contrary to the laws of the State, with a slave or free negro, or shall suffer any slave or free negro to play at a game, or bet at a gaming table, or to wager money or other valuable thing contrary to the laws of the State, on his or her premises, or on any premises under his or her control, shall on conviction be fined fifty dollars for each offence.

The informer shall receive one-half the fine imposed. § 118.—One half of the fine imposed against any person for the violation of either of the two preceding sections shall be paid to the informer, and if there be no informer, then it shall be paid to the officer making the arrest.

Houses of ill-fame.

Penalty. § 119.—Every person, who shall keep a disorderly house, or a house of ill-fame within the limits of the city, shall upon conviction before the Mayor or an Alderman be fined in the sum of fifty dollars, and upon failure to pay the fine and costs, such person shall be committed to jail until the said fine and costs are paid, but in no case shall the imprisonment exceed sixty days.

Persons continuing to keep houses of ill-fame. § 120.—Every person, who shall keep a house of ill-fame after being once convicted thereof, for each and every day he or she shall continue to keep such a house of ill-fame, shall be fined fifty dollars, *shall be fined.* and upon default of payment thereof, shall be committed to jail until said fine and costs are paid, but in no case shall the imprisonment exceed sixty days.

§ 121.—Any house, inhabited by disorderly or lewd women, or persons of bad reputation as to chastity, or frequented by persons for the purpose of prostitution, shall be considered a house of ill-fame, and all adults living in such a house shall be considered the keepers thereof, and subject to the penalties imposed by this code upon such an offence. *Any house inhabited by lewd women sh'll be considered a house of ill-fame*

§ 122.—Any person having the control of a dwelling or other building within the city who shall rent it, or permit it to be used as a house of ill-fame, shall on conviction before the Mayor or an Alderman, be fined fifty dollars, and on failing to pay the fine, such person shall be committed to jail until the fine and costs are paid, but in no case shall the imprisonment exceed sixty days. *Any person renting a building to be used as house of ill-fame shall be fined.*

§ 123.—Every person who shall interrupt or disturb any assembly convened for the purpose of religious worship, shall be fined fifty dollars for each offence. *Interrupting public worship.*

§ 124.—Every proprietor of a public house of any kind, who shall permit any person at such a house, to disturb the peace or quiet of the neighborhood by loud singing or any noisy and disorderly conduct, shall be fined ten dollars. *The proprietor of a public house permitting disorderly conduct, shall be fined.*

§ 125.—Every person who shall injure or deface any public building by cutting or breaking or drawing or writing upon the walls thereof, shall on conviction be fined five dollars for each offence. *Defacing a public building.*

§ 126.—Every person, who shall cut, break, or disfigure the walls of public buildings, or cut, break or remove trees, shrubs, grass, gravel, or dirt, *Removing trees, shrubs &c., from public grounds.*

50

from the public grounds shall be fined five dollars, for each offence.

Injuring the property of the city. § 127.—Every person who shall break the lamps or posts of any property of the city, or shall injure the fences enclosing a public building, shall be fined five dollars, for each offence.

Hitching an animal to a public building or fence. § 128.—Every person, who shall hitch an animal to a public building, or to the fence around such building or to the lamp posts of the city, shall be fined five dollars.

Shooting a gun or pistol. § 129.—Every person, who shall shoot or discharge a gun, pistol, or any kind of fire-arms within the limits of the city, shall be fined five dollars

The preceding section does not apply to Military corps &c. § 130.—The provisions of the preceding section shall not apply to persons defending themselves or their property, nor to military companies.

CHAPTER XII.

EXCAVATION OF CELLARS, &c.

Excavation for any purpose forbidden in months of July, August, or September. § 131.—Every person, who shall excavate a cellar, or dig out dirt for the purpose of building, or for any other purpose during the months of July, August or September, shall be fined ten dollars; and the additional sum of five dollars for every day after conviction such person shall violate this section.

No person shall dig river banks or streets. &c. § 132.—Any person, who shall dig, cut, or carry away any part of the banks of the river, or commons, or streets, or dig or carry away dirt from any land owned by the city, without the permission of the City Council, shall be fined five dollars.

A slave or free negro violating § 133.—Any slave or free negro, violating the foregoing section, shall receive not more than twenty lashes, which punishment may be commuted to a fine of not more than ten dollars, according to the discretion of the person before whom the case may be tried.

foregoin section.

—

CHAPTER XIII.

EXHIBITIONS, LECTURES, AND THEATRES.

§ 134.—Every person who shall lecture, open a theatre, or give a concert or an exhibition of any kind for money, without a license for which the sum of five dollars shall be paid for each day or night such exhibition may continue, shall be fined twenty dollars.

All persons who lectues or give exhibition for money must obtain a license:

§ 135.—Every person who shall open a circus, or a show of animals without a license for which twenty dollars shall be paid, for each performance or exhibition, shall be fined forty dollars.

Circuses and menageries must obtain licenses.

§ 136.—No license shall be required to exhibit paintings, statuary, or a useful invention, or for an exhibition or entertainment intended only to promote religious or charitable objects.

Exhibitions for charitable purposes.

§ 137.—The Marshal or a policeman, shall attend all exhitions or entertainments free of charge, and demand the license granted by the Clerk; and on failure of the persons giving the exhibition to show the license, the Marshal or policeman shall arrest and carry such persons before the Mayor or an Alderman for trial.

The Marshal shall attend all exhibitions, and demand license.

§ 138.—The Clerk or Marshal or policeman failing to discharge his duties as above prescribed, shall be fined ten dollars.

The Clerk or Marshal failing to perform his duty fined

CHAPTER XIV.

FINES AND FEES.

Persons failing to pay a fine shall be imprisoned.

§ 139.—All persons failing to pay the fine imposed on them for the violation of a law of the city, shall be committed to prison until the fine and costs are paid, but in no case shall the imprisonment exceed sixty days.

The Mayor or Alderman may issue an execution for the fine, &c.

§ 140.—The Mayor or Alderman before whom the case is tried, may issue an execution for the amount of fine and costs, which shall be levied by the Marshal, on any property belonging to the person convicted of a breach of a law of the city.

Property levied on to collect a fine.

Real estate levied on.

§ 141.—When an execution is levied on personal property to enforce the payment of a fine, the Marshal shall advertise in a newspaper, the property, the time and place of sale for at least ten days before such sale shall be made; and when an execution is levied on real estate, the Marshal shall insert such an advertisement for at least thirty successive days, before the day of sale.

On payment of fine, the Marshall shall mark the docket, "satisfied."

§ 142.—On the payment of the fine and costs by any person, the Marshal shall mark the case "satisfied" on the docket, and if required, shall also give a receipt to the person making the payment.

Complaint of a citizen.

§ 143.—The Mayor, upon the complaint of a citizen that a person has violated a law of the city, shall issue a summons commanding the Marshal or other officer to arrest the accused, and to bring him or her before the Mayor at an appointed time to answer the allegations of the complaint, which must be clearly and specifically stated.

Any person arrested upon complaint of another, may

§ 144.—Any person, arrested upon the complaint of another, may give bond for not less than one hundred, nor more than two hundred dollars, for

53

his appearance before the Mayor at the appointed time, and on failure to do so, such person shall be committed to prison until the case can be tried.

give bond. &c.

§ 145.—Every person tried on the complaint of another, and convicted of having broken the laws of the city shall be punished according to the provisions of the law violated, but if he or she be acquitted, all the costs of the case shall be paid by the person making the complaint.

Any person convicted shall be punished: if acquitted, the person making complaint must pay costs.

§ 146.—The Marshal, or any other officer of the city, shall summon all the witnesses whose attendance is required, at any trial before the Mayor, an Alderman, or the City Council.

The Marshal shall summon all witnesses.

§ 147.—Any witness, who, without a sufficient excuse, shall fail to attend at the time stated in the summons, shall be fined ten dollars, and on failure to pay the fine, shall be committed to prison not exceeding ten days.

Any witness failing to attend shall be fined.

§ 148.—Any person summoned as a witness before the Mayor, an Alderman, or the City Council, who shall refuse to answer all proper questions, shall be committed to jail until he or she is willing to testify.

Any person refusing to testify shall be imprisoned.

§ 149.—The costs in every case tried before the Mayor or an Alderman, shall be entered upon the trial docket, and collected by the City Marshal; and in no case shall the Mayor or Marshal be entitled to any fees, unless such fees are clearly set down, item by item, on the docket.

The costs in every case shall be entered on the trial docket.

§ 150.—The Mayor shall be entitled to the following fees herein mentioned :

The fees of the Mayor.

For every license granted by him, under the ordinances of the city,...........................$1 00

For every case tried before him,.................. 1 00

For every execution to enforce the collection of fines or taxes,.................................... 50

§ 151.—In every case tried before the Mayor, in which the accused shall be acquitted, or the person convicted shall be insolvent, the City Treasurer, with the consent of the City Council, shall pay to the Mayor the fees above stated.

The fees of the Mayor, how paid.

§ 152.—The Clerk and Marshal shall receive the following fees:

The fees of the Clerk and Marshal.

The Clerk, for every license issued by him, unless otherwise provided, shall be paid.............$1 00
For levying an execution, ... 1 00
For making deed to real estate, sold for taxes, 2 00
For bill of sale for personal property,......... 1 00
For issuing subpœna for witness,.............. 25
The Marshal shall receive for arresting a free person... 2 00
The Marshal shall receive for arresting a slave 1 00
For summoning each witness,................... 25
For taking bond of any person arrested,...... 1 00

But in no case shall the fees above mentioned be paid to the Clerk or the marshal, if the person tried for an offence be acquitted, or being convicted shall be insolvent.

If the person be acquitted or insolvent the fees shall not be paid.

CHAPTER XV.

THE FIRE DEPARTMENT—FIRE LIMITS.

The organization of the Fire Department.

§ 153.—The Dexter Fire Company, number one; the Alabama Fire Company, number two; and the Mechanics' Hook and Ladder Company, number one, and such other companies as may be organized hereafter and received into the Department by the City Council, shall constitute, and be known as, the Fire Department of the city of Montgomery.

§ 154.—The Fire Department shall have for its officers one Chief Engineer and three Assistant Engineers, who shall be elected in the month of January in each year, and hold their offices for the term of one year, and until their successors are chosen and qualified.

The officers of the Fire Department

§ 155.—The Chief and Assistant Engineers shall be elected in the following manner, viz: each Company, composing the Department, shall nominate a candidate for each office, and the City Council shall elect from the persons so nominated, and the person receiving a majority of the votes cast, shall be declared elected.

The mode of electing the Chief and Assistant Engineers.

§ 156.—Before entering upon the duties of their respective offices, the Chief Engineer, and each Assistant Engineer, shall make the following oath before the Mayor: "I, ——, do solemnly swear that I will faithfully observe the laws of the State of Alabama, and the ordinances of the city, and to the best of my ability perform the duties of my office."

The oath of the Chief Engineer and his Assistants.

§ 157.—The officers of the Fire Department, or any one of them, may be removed at any time by the City Council.

The officers may be removed by the Council.

§ 158.—If a vacancy occurs in any of the offices during the year, the Mayor shall notify the companies of the Department, and the office shall be filled in the same manner as at the annual election.

Vacancy in any office shall be filled as at the annual election.

§ 159.—The city shall be divided into three Districts as follows; District number one, shall be composed of wards, one and two; District number two, of wards, three and four; District number three, of wards, five and six; the Assistant Engineers shall be chosen, one from each District.

The division of the city into districts.

56

The hat of the Engineers.

§ 160.—Each of the Engineers shall wear a hat similar in form to that now worn by Engine Companies one and two, made of white leather with a black front, and having their respective offices marked on it; each of them shall also carry a speaking trumpet.

The Chief Engineers shall control the companies at fires.

§ 161.—The Chief Engineer in all cases of fire, shall have sole control of every company, belonging to the Fire Department, and of all the engines and apparatus belonging thereto; and any officer of a company, refusing or neglecting to obey a lawful order of said Engineer, may be fined in a sum

Penalty for refusing to obey him.

not exceeding twenty-five dollars upon conviction thereof, before the Mayor or Alderman.

All white persons when called upon to assist in extinguishing a fire shall do so.

§ 162.—All white persons present at a fire shall give aid in suppressing it, when called upon to do so, by any officer of the Fire Department, or by an officer of a company belonging to the department; and any one, refusing or neglecting to render such

Penalty for refusing.

assistance, shall, upon conviction thereof, before the Mayor or an Alderman, be fined not more than

Negroes refusing shall be whipped.

twenty dollars; and any negro refusing or neglecting so to do, shall receive not more than thirty-nine stripes.

The Engineers shall be Marshals of the city.

§ 163.—The Chief Engineer and the assistant Engineers at fires, shall be marshals of the City, *ex-officio.*

Buildings or fires may be blown up or removed by order of Chief Engineer.

§ 164.—To prevent the spread of fire, the Chief Engineer upon consultation with one or more of the Assistant Engineers, with as many of the foremen of the Companies as practicable, and with the Mayor, if he be present or near the place of fire, may order any building or fence to be blown up or

Proviso.

otherwise removed, *provided*, such order shall receive the sanction of a majority of those consulted.

The Chief Engineer

§ 165.—The Chief Engineer shall provide for

the keeping of the apparatus of the companies of this Department in good order, and at all times ready for immediate use. But in discharging this duty, he shall not contract a debt to be paid by the City Council for the repairs of the apparatus, or of the building in which it is kept, exceeding fifty dollars. Any repairs which require a larger sum of money shall be referred to the City Council.

shall provide for the keeping of the apparatus, &c.

§ 166.—The Chief Engineer shall keep a correct account of the fires, and alarms of fire, their cause, and the amount of property destroyed, during his term of office, and report the same to the City Council in January of every year.

Chief Engineer must report number of fires, and amount of property destroyed.

§ 167.—The Chief Engineer shall make, in the month of January of every year, a report to the City Council of the number of companies, belonging to the department, the number of members in each company, and the condition of the apparatus and buildings in possession of the companies, together with any information in connection with his office, which may be beneficial to the city or the Department.

Chief Engineer must report number of Companies, condition of apparatus, &c.

§ 168.—The Chief Engineer, and his Assistants, shall ascertain, in case of fire, where water can be obtained for the use of the engines, and inform the foreman of each company.

Chief and Ass't. Engineers must ascertain where water may be found.

§ 169.—The Assistant Engineers shall convey the orders of the Chief Engineer to the officers of the different companies, aid in the proper execution of them, and perform all other duties which he may require of them. In the absence of the Chief Engineer, the first Assitant Engineer, and in his absence the second Assistant Engineer, and in his absence the third Assistant Engineer, and in the absence of all the Engineers, the Foreman of the Company first arriving at the fire, shall have

Duties of Assistant Engineers.

In the absence of all Engineers, &c.

the authority and perform the duties of Chief Engineer.

Meetings of the Engineers must be held every three months. § 170.—A meeting shall be held, at least once in every three months, by the Chief Engineer, the Assistant Engineers, and two representatives from 'each Company, for the purpose of considering the condition of the Companies, and adopting such measures as will insure the greatest efficiency in this Department.

Fire limits of the city. § 171.—The Fire limits of the city of Montgomery shall be McDonough street, on the east, Washington street on the south and south-west, the Alabama river on the west, Madison street on the north, and Coosa street on the north-west.

No wooden building to be erected therein. § 172.—No person shall build any wooden house, shed or other structure of wood within the above described fire limits; and any person so doing, shall be fined ten dollars on **Penalty.** conviction thereof, and five dollars for every day thereafter this section shall be violated; *Provided,* a reasonable time shall have been allowed for a compliance with this section.

What shall be considered a wooden building. § 173.—Every building which shall be erected with more wood on its outside than is required, for door and window frames, roof, eaves, cornices, doors, shutters, sash, porticoes and steps to the first floor above ground, shall be considered a wooden building; and all having a wooden frame work to be covered with tin, zinc or other material shall be also considered wooden buildings.

Wooden buildings outside the fire limits must not be carried within them without permission, &c. § 174.—No person shall carry any wooden building outside the fire limits to any lot within them, nor move any wooden building within the fire limits from one place to another, without first obtaining the permission of the City Council, and the consent of the owners of the adjoining lots, and any person, who shall violate this section, shall be fined ten dollars, and five dollars for every day thereafter the violation of this section shall continue.

§ 175.—Every person, who shall, without the consent of the City Council set up a steam engine, a foundry, a blacksmith shop, a bakery, an establishment for boiling soap, or any similar establishment, in any building, other than a brick building, having a slate or metal roof, shall be fined twenty dollars for every day this section shall be violated.

§ 176.—Any person who shall use a building for a plank or lumber kiln without the permission of the City Council, shall be fined twenty dollars.

§ 177.—Every person who shall enlarge or elevate a wooden building of any kind within the Fire limits, or cover the roof of a building in the Fire limits with any material other than tin, slate, zink, tile or some incombustible composition shall be fined ten dollars, and five dollars for every day thereafter this section shall be violated.

Penalty.

No person, without consent of Council, shall set up a foundry, &c.

No person, without consent of City Council, shall use a building for lumber kiln

No person shall enlarge a wooden building or cover a roof with combustible material &c.

CHAPTER XVI.

HEALTH, HOSPITAL, AND CITY PHYSICIAN.

§ 178.—The City Council shall appoint, when necessary, two persons from each ward of the city, who, with the Mayor, shall constitute a Board of Health, of which the Mayor shall be the President.

§ 179.—The Mayor, as the President, or in company with other members of the Board of Health, shall inspect all lots, and cause the removal of any

Board of Health established.

The Mayor shall inspect all lots, &c.

matter on such lots which may become a nuisance, or have a tendency to injure the health of the citizens.

Mayor must examine the condition of the city.

§ 180.—The Mayor shall, personally, ascertain the sanitary condition of the city, and report at least once a month to the City Council.

During epidemics the Mayor must report daily

§ 181.—During the prevalence of epidemics, the Mayor shall, as the President of the Board of Health, make daily reports of the health of the city, for the truth and correctness of which he shall be held responsible to the City Council. The President can call a meeting of the Board of Health, whenever he may consider it necessary.

Every owner or occupant must keep their premises in good condition.

§ 182.—Every owner or agent or occupant of any house, yard or lot in the city, shall keep it clean, and not permit anything calculated to generate disease to remain on the premises.

Persons refusing to obey orders of Board of Health fined.

§ 183.—Every person, who fails or refuses to comply with the orders of the Mayor or Board of Health, shall be fined on conviction thereof, before the Mayor or an Alderman, in the sum of twenty dollars, for every such offence.

The marshal shall execute the orders of the Board of Health.

§ 184.—The Marshal shall execute the orders of the Mayor or Board of Health, and the cost of doing so, shall be taxed against the owner or occupant of the premises, and shall be collected by the marshal.

Persons aggrieved by action of Board of Health may appeal to the Council.

§ 185.—Every person aggrieved by the action of the Mayor or the Board of Health, upon notifying the Mayor in writing of his or her intention, shall have the right to appeal to the City Council; upon receiving such notice, the Mayor shall suspend the proceedings of the Board of Health, until the cause is heard and determined by the City Council, and their decision shall control the action of the Mayor or Board of Health in the case.

§ 186.—The marshal and every member of the City Police in addition to the duties already performed by them, shall diligently search for, and report to the Mayor anything which will endanger the public health.

§ 187.—Every person who shall empty upon the side-walks, or streets, or into the ditches, sewers or drains of the city, any feculent matter, filth or liquid, emitting a noisome odor, or injurious to health, shall be fined five dollars for each offence.

§ 188.—Every owner, overseer or manager of any slave, afflicted with the small pox, who shall fail to remove such slave to the city hospital within twenty-four hours after the appearance of the disease, shall on conviction before the Mayor or an Alderman, be fined fifty dollars, and the further sum of fifty dollars for each day thereafter, the owner, manager, or overseer shall neglect or refuse to remove the diseased slave to the city hospital.

§ 189.—Upon the neglect or refusal of the owner, manager or overseer of any slave diseased with the small pox to remove the slave, the marshal or deputy marshal shall cause the slave to be carried to the hospital at the expense of the owner, or the person controlling the slave.

§ 190.—Any owner or manager of a slave, having the small pox, who shall fail or refuse to pay the cost of removing the slave to the city hospital upon the request of the marshal, shall be fined ten dollars.

§ 191.—Any physician, having a patient within the limits of the city, afflicted with the small pox, who shall fail for the space of twenty-four hours, to report the name and residence of the patient to the ¡President of the Board of Health, shall be fined for every such patient the sum of fifty dollars.

§ 192.—No person shall be permitted to reside in the City Hospital, nor shall any one be maintained at the expense of the city, unless such person be disqualified by disease from gaining a livelihood.

§ 193.—No person shall be admitted into the hospital without a written certificate from the city physician, specifying the character of the disease ; and upon the presentation of the certificate the steward shall receive the person into the hospital.

§ 194.—The Hospital steward shall live in the hospital, and shall take charge of all the furniture, beds, bedding, clothes and cooking utensils, and keep them clean and in good order, and subject at all times to the inspection of the Mayor, Aldermen or marshal. The steward shall also keep an inventory of all articles belonging to the city, in his possession ; and shall report to the City Council, all the stores received by him for the use of the hospital.

§ 195.—The steward shall register the name of all persons, admitted into the hospital, their native place, sex, age, occupation, the time of admission to the hospital, and time of discharge or death. He shall nurse the patients, provide, and prepare such food for them as the city physician may prescribe.

§ 196.—No person shall be permitted to remain in or about the hospital, unless lawfully admitted as a patient, nor shall any person remain in the hospital after being discharged by the city physician.

§ 197.—No alcoholic or intoxicating liquors of any description, shall be carried to the hospital premises, except by order of the city physician. kept about the premises.

§ 198.—The Steward shall keep the grounds around the hospital in good condition. He shall always preserve order in the hospital, and report the improper conduct of patients or other persons to the city physician, the Mayor or marshal. The Steward must keep the grounds in good order, &c.

§ 199.—The City Council shall elect, annually, a City Physician, who shall hold his office for twelve months, and until his successor is chosen, unless sooner removed, and shall receive such compensation as the City Council may appoint. He may be removed from his office at any time by the City Council for neglect of duty or improper conduct. A City Physician shall be elected annually.

§ 200.—The City Physician shall examine all applicants for admission into the city hospital, and grant certificates to such as may be worthy to be admitted. He shall keep a register of the names of the patients, their native place, sex, age, occupation, time of admission and time of discharge or death, and shall describe the disease of each patient, its nature, progress and termination. The register kept, shall be subject at all times to the inspection of the Mayor or any Alderman. The duties of the City Physician.

§ 201.—The City Physician shall visit the hospital as often as the condition of the patients may require, and prescribe such medicine, diet and general treatment as may be necessary; he shall also inspect the hospital, and report any neglect or mismanagement of the steward or any improper conduct of the inmates to the Mayor. City Physician shall visit the hospital and prescribe for the patients.

§ 202.—Every person controlling a steamboat, or a conductor upon the cars of a railroad or any other person who shall bring or assist in bringing to the city any person having a contagious disease, No person having a contagious disease shall be brought to the city.

or is disabled in any manner, or is incapable of earning a livelihood shall be fined fifty dollars.

Persons intending to support invalids may bring them to the city. § 203.—The foregoing section shall not apply to any person bringing to the city a disabled or diseased person, not sick with a contagious disease, who will support such invalids at his or her own expense.

CHAPTER XVII.

LICENSES.

All licenses shall expire on 1st day of March. § 204.—All licenses, issued by authority of the City Council, shall expire on the first day of March next after the issuance thereof, unless otherwise provided.

No license shall be issued for less time than a year. § 205.—No license shall be issued for a less time than one year, unless the applicant for the license, shall have engaged in business after the first day of March, then such person shall pay for the license according to the time it will continue. But no license shall be granted to peddlers or itinerant persons, authorizing them to sell by sample or otherwise, for less time than one year.

Hawking or pedling goods, wares and merchandise on the streets. § 206.—Every person who shall hawk or peddle about the streets of the city, goods, wares, or merchandise, or offer them for sale by sample or otherwise, without a license authorized by the City Council for which the sum of twenty-five dollars shall be paid ,shall be fined not less than twenty-five, nor more than fifty dollars.

Selling fruit, poultry, &c. § 207.—The preceding section shall not apply to any person selling fruit, vegetables, poultry, eggs, corn, fodder, oats, hay, or any article produced or manufactured by him or her in this State.

§. 208.—All persons or firms engaging in business as auctioneers, or selling, hiring or renting, or offering for sale, hire or rent within the limits of the city, any property belonging to another person, without a license for which the sum of fifty dollars shall be paid, shall be fined twenty dollars for each offence.

Auctioneers or persons selling or hiring property.

§ 209.—The preceding section shall, in no manner apply to sales under execution, or by order of court, or under a mortgage, or by executors, administrators or guardians.

Officer of Court. Executors, &c., need no license.

§ 210.—Every commission merchant, and all factors, or brokers, who shall carry on business in the city without a license for which fifty dollars shall be paid, shall be fined not less than ten, nor more than fifty dollars.

Commission Merchants, Factors, &c.

§ 211.—Every person who shall keep a warehouse for the storage of cotton or other produce, or any article of value without a license for which one hundred dollars shall be paid, shall be fined not less than twenty-five, nor more than fifty dollars.

Warehouse keepers.

§ 212.—Any Insurance Company, which shall open an office or engage in business in the city without a license, for which fifty dollars shall be paid, shall be fined not less than twenty-five, nor more than fifty dollars.

Insurance Companies.

§ 213.—Every company engaged in the manufacture of gas without a license for which the sum of one hundred dollars shall be paid, in addition to the tax which may be levied on the property so employed, shall be fined not less than twenty-five, nor more than fifty dollars.

Gas Company.

§ 214.—Every person, who shall open a lottery office, or sell lottery tickets within the limits of the city, without a license, for which two hundred dollars shall be paid, shall be fined any sum not exceeding fifty dollars.

Lottery Agents.

Free Banks or Bank Agencies.

§ 215.—Every free bank or bank agency, which shall engage in business without a license, for which one hundred dollars shall be paid, shall be fined in any sum not exceeding fifty dollars.

Brokers or Exchange Dealers.

§ 216.—Every person, who shall engage in business as a broker or exchange dealer without a license, for which fifty dollars shall be paid, shall be fined not less than ten, nor more than fifty dollars.

Keepers of a Livery Stable shall obtain a license.

§ 217.—Every person who shall open a livery stable, or a stable for the sale of horses, mules, or stock of any kind without a license for which fifty dollars shall be paid, shall, after being notified of this section, be fined twenty dollars for each day, such person shall neglect to obtain a license.

Selling horses and mules without license.

§ 218.—Any person, except the proprietor of a livery stable, who shall bring horses or mules to market and offer them for sale without a license for which one dollar, for each animal, shall be paid, shall be fined not less than ten nor more than fifty dollars.

Money paid for license to sell horses or mules refunded if no sale.

§ 219.—If any person having obtained a license according to the terms of the preceding section should carry away any animals, which were brought by him to market, then one dollar for each animal, remaining unsold, shall be returned to its owner or his agent.

All persons engaging in mercantile business shall obtain license.

§ 220.—Every person, who shall sell or barter goods, wares, or merchandise, or keep a cake, candy or fruit store, or engage in any mercantile business, without a license for which twenty-five dollars shall be paid, shall, after being notified of this section, be fined twenty dollars for each day, such person shall neglect to obtain a licence.

Persons selling flour, bacon, &c., from a wagon must ob-

§ 221.—Any person, who shall sell from a wagon or other vehicle, bacon, flour, tobacco or similar articles at retail without a license for which ten dollars shall be paid, shall be fined not less than five, nor more than twenty dollars.

§ 222.—Every person, who shall play in the streets on any musical instrument for money without a license, for which the sum of ten dollars shall be paid, shall be fined five dollars for each offence.

tain license.

Musicians playing on the streets shall obtain a license.

§ 223.—Every person, who shall keep a tavern or hotel without a license, for which fifty dollars shall be paid, shall be fined not less than five, nor more than fifty dollars.

Keepers of taverns, &c. shall obtain a license.

§ 224.—Every person, who shall keep a restaurant without a license, for which twenty-five dollars shall be paid, shall be fined not less than five, nor more than twenty-five dollars.

Licenses for keeping Restaurat.

§ 225.—Every person, who shall keep a public billiard table for hire, without a license for which one hundred dollars shall be paid, shall be fined twenty-five dollars for each day such person shall neglect to obtain a license.

Billiard table shall not be kept without license.

§ 226.—Every person, who shall keep a public bagatelle or pool table, or any other table, or stand for gaming without a license, for which one hundred dollars shall be paid, shall be fined twenty dollars.

License shall be obtained by owners of public pool tables, &c.

§ 227.—Every person, who shall keep a pistol gallery without a license, for which fifty dollars shall be paid, shall be fined not less than ten, nor more than fifty dollars.

Pistol gallery.

§ 228.—Every person, who shall keep a public ten pin alley, or alley of like kind without a license, for which fifty dollars shall be paid, shall be fined thirty dollars.

Tenpin alleys must have license

§ 229.—All licenses for day laborers, washerwomen or barbers, shall expire on the first day of February, in every year, and shall date from the first day of February, May, August or November; and the

Licenses for daily laborers and barbers.

applicant for such a license shall pay in proportion to the time the license will continue.

CHAPTER XVIII.

MAGAZINE.

Clerk of the Magazine. § 230.—The City Council shall appoint annually a clerk of the magazine.

Clerk shall give a bond, &c. § 231.—The clerk of the magazine immediately after his election, shall give a bond with sureties for one thousand dollars for the faithful performance of the duties of his office.

Salary of the Clerk. § 232.—The City Council, shall fix a salary for the clerk of the magazine, at the time of his election, which shall not be increased or diminished during the term of his office.

The Clerk shall attend his office. § 233.—The clerk shall keep his office near the centre of the city, and he shall, at all hours between sunrise and sunset, receive powder into the magazine, or deliver it from the magazine according to the request of the owners or their agent.

A tax upon powder. § 234.—A tax of twenty-five cents upon every keg, and fifteen cents for every half keg of powder stored in the magazine, shall be collected by the clerk on the delivery of the powder to its owner.

The tax shall be paid to the Treasurer. § 235.—The taxes so collected, shall be paid over to the city treasurer by the clerk of the magazine, who shall render an account of the money obtained at any time the City Council may require him so to do.

The Clerk neglecting his duties, discharged. § 236.—The clerk of the magazine neglecting or refusing to discharge his duties promptly, shall on conviction before the City Council, be fined ten dollars, or be dismissed from his office, or be fined and dismissed according to the discretion of the City Council.

§ 237.—Every person who shall keep more than one keg of powder in his store, or in any place, other than the City Magazine, shall on conviction, be fined twenty dollars for every such offence.

No person shall keep more than one keg of powder.

CHAPTER XIX.

MARKET, MEASURES AND SCALES.

§ 238.—The Market shall be divided into stalls, which shall be numbered and rented to the highest bidder for cash, at twelve o'clock, M., on the first Monday in the month of February, of every year; but in no case shall the stalls be rented at less than the following rates: for each of the four butcher's stalls in the east end of the market, one hundred dollars; for each of the four stalls in the middle of the market, eighty dollars; for each of the stalls for the sale of vegetables, twenty-five dollars, and for each coffee stand, fifty dollars.

The Market shall be divided into stalls, and rented annually.

The stalls shall not be rented for less than one hundred dollars, &c.

§ 239.—Any person renting more stalls than are necessary for carrying on his or her business, shall not have the power to underlet such stalls, and shall be fined ten dollars for each day such person shall retain control of the stall.

No person shall rent more stalls than are necessary for his business.

§ 240.—The City Council, at its first meeting in the month of February, of each year, shall elect a Market Clerk, who shall remain in office for the space of one year, unless sooner dismissed by the City Council.

Market Clerk.

§ 241.—The City Council electing the market clerk shall fix the amount of his salary before his election, and it shall not be diminished during his term of office.

§ 242.—Market hours shall begin half an hour before daylight, and end at nine o'clock, A. M., from the first day of October until the first day of April ; and half an hour before day-light, and end at eight o'clock, A. M., from first day of April till the first day of October of every year, but on every Saturday, the market shall remain open all day.

§ 243.—The clerk of the market shall remain there during market hours, regulate the weights and measures according to the standard adopted by the city, decide all disputes between buyers and sellers, and collect the fees accruing to the city from the market.

§ 244.—The clerk shall exercise a general supervision over the market , and he is hereby authorized to arrest all persons who fight, or are guilty of any indecent or disorderly conduct.

§ 245.—The clerk, for the purpose of preserving peace and good order, is empowered to call upon any citizen to aid him, and any person refusing his assistance, shall on conviction be fined five dollars.

§ 246.—The clerk shall exclude from the market square during market hours, all vehicles or animals not bringing provisions for sale, and shall kill all dogs near enough to annoy or injure persons attending market.

§ 247.—The clerk shall condemn all unsound and unwholesome provisions brought to the market for sale, and have them immediately removed and destroyed ; and any person resisting or disobeying the

Marginal notes:

Salary of the Market Clerk.

Market hours.

The Clerk shall remain there during the market hours.

General superintendence of the market, &c.

The Clerk to preserve peace.

Vehicles and dogs shall be excluded from market square.

Unsound provisions.

71

clerk, shall on conviction be fined not exceeding twenty-five dollars.

§ 248.—Any person, who shall during market hours buy provisions for the purpose of speculating, shall be reported by the Clerk, and, on conviction, shall be fined twenty dollars for each offence.

No person during market shall buy provisions for speculation.

§ 249.—Any person, who shall hawk about the streets, or sell fruit, vegetables, poultry, eggs, or table supplies after nine o'clock on Sunday, shall be fined ten dollars.

No person shall hawk vegetables about the streets on Sunday.

§ 250.—The clerk shall prevent the obstruction of the side walks, and allow all persons an opportunity of selling their produce ; he shall also permit those first arriving to choose their place on the market square.

The side-walks shall not be obstructed.

§ 251.—The clerk shall ring the market bell for at least one minute at the close of market hours, and shall have the market house except the rented stalls swept, and kept in good order.

The close of market house.

§ 252.—At the close of the market hours, the lessees of the stalls, shall have the stalls, benches, tables, cutting blocks and scales swept, scraped and thoroughly cleaned, and any lessee violating this section, shall be reported by the clerk, and on conviction, shall be fined five dollars.

The market house must be thoroughly cleaned.

§ 253.—If upon the complaint of any person, the clerk shall be convicted of neglecting his duties, or showing partiality, or making an unjust order to any one, or failing to execute the laws governing the market, he shall be fined twenty-five dollars or dismissed, according to the discretion of the City Council.

Misconduct of the Clerk.

§ 254.—All measures, weights, and balances, used in the city, shall conform to the standard adopted by the State, and a complete set of them, shall be kept by the city clerk.

Measures, weights, &c.

§ 255.—Every person, selling or buying by measures, weight or balances, not conforming to the standard above mentioned, shall be fined five dollars for each offence.

§ 256.—Every person, who shall fraudulently use false measures, weights, or balances, in buying or selling, shall, on conviction, be fined fifty dollars.

§ 257.—Any person, who shall sell any article of merchandise by a false mark, brand, number or device, or knowingly sell falsely packed flour or sugar, or other articles, shall on conviction be fined fifty dollars.

§ 258.—The city clerk or marshal, at the request of a citizen, shall test any measure, weight or balance by the city standard, and brand it with some uniform letter or device for which service the clerk or marshal shall be paid fifty cents.

§ 259.—The City Council shall provide suitable scales and weights for the use of the public, upon which, at the request of any person, shall be weighed articles of produce or merchandise by the public weigher.

§ 260.—The City Council shall appoint annually a public weigher and pay him a salary which shall not be diminished during his term of office.

§ 261.—The public weigher shall give a bond with good sureties in the sum of three thousand dollars for the faithful performance of his duties; for the delivery of all money collected by him to the City Treasurer, and for the payment of all damages incurred by any person on account of his negligence or carelessness in the discharge of his duties.

§ 262.—Before entering upon the duties of his office, the public weigher, in addition to his bond, shall make and subscribe the following affidavit, which

Margin notes: Weights not conforming to the standard. Persons fraudulently using false weights fined. False mark, brand, &c. Testing the weights, measures, &c., by city standard. Public scales. A public weigher. The bond of public weigher. The oath of public weigher.

be filed with the City Clerk: "I —— do solemnly swear that I will discharge the duties of public weigher of the city of Montgomery, to the best of my ability, and will show no partiality during my term of office.

§ 263.—The public weigher shall keep the scales and apparatus in good condition, and weigh without delay, coal, lime, bacon, corn, fodder, oats, hay, and any produce or merchandise brought to market, and sold by weight or measurement from wagons or other vehicles on the streets; for which he shall be paid by the purchaser of the articles the following rates, viz: For every load on a vehicle with four wheels, drawn by four or more animals, fifty cents; for every load on a vehicle with four wheels drawn by any number of animals less than four, twenty-five cents; for every load on a vehicle with two wheels, drawn by any number of animals, twenty-five cents. *The duties of the public weigher.* *Rates charged for weighing.*

§ 264.—The public weigher, when required by the City Council or Mayor, shall examine any or all measures, weights, scales or balances, used in the city, in the sale or purchase of goods, wares, and merchandise, and report any variance from the city standard to the Mayor, and any person refusing to produce his or her measures, weights, scales, or balances for inspection or interrupting the weigher in the discharge of his duty, shall be fined fifty dollars. *The public weigher shall inspect measures, weights and scales.*

§ 265.—No person shall erect public scales on any of the streets, and every person who shall keep public scales or weigh for the public any merchandise or produce except cotton, sold from wagons or other vehicles on the streets, without a license, for which twenty-five dollars shall be paid shall be fined, not less than five, nor more than twenty-five dollars. *No person shall keep public scales without license.*

§ 266.—Every licensed weigher shall keep at all times between sunrise and sunset of ea   day, Sunday excepted, a competent white person in attendance on the scales, and any one violating this section, shall be fined twenty dollars.

A white person shall aways be at the scales.

§ 267.—Every licensed weigher shall be authorized to charge and collect the same rates, charged by the public weigher of the city, and any one violating this section, shall be fined fifty dollars.

Licensed weigher, charges.

§ 268.—Every bushel of shelled corn sold in the city from the first day of December till the first day of September next thereafter, shall contain fifty-six pounds; every bushel of corn in the ear, sixty-four pounds, and every bushel of corn in the ear, not husked seventy-three pounds; and from the first day of September until the first day of December next thereafter, every bushel of unhusked corn shall weigh seventy-four pounds, and every bushel of husked corn in the ear, sixty-five pounds; any licensed weigher, violating in any manner this section, shall be fined twenty dollars.

The weight of corn.

CHAPTER XX.

NUISANCE.

§ 269.—Every person, who shall make a tanyard, slaughter house, or butcher pen, or engage in any business which will injure the adjoining property, or affect the health or comfort of the people, shall be fined twenty dollars for each day the nuisance shall continue.

Tan yard, &c

§ 270.—If the owner of the nuisance shall fail to remove it, the City Council shall order it to be

Failing to abate the nuisance.

abated at the cost of the person causing the nuisance.

§ 271.—If the person causing the nuisance be insolvent or unable to pay the cost of its removal, or absconds, then the cost of abating the nuisance, shall be taxed against the property on which it was situated, and be collected at the same time, and in the same manner as the annual taxes.

If the person be insolvent or absconds, the cost of removal shall be taxed.

CHAPTER XXI.

PAUPERS.

§ 272.—Every one who shall bring or cause to be brought to the city, a person having no means of support, and unable or unwilling to work, with the intent of making such person a charge upon the city, or on the charity of the citizens, shall be fined not exceeding fifty dollars for each day, such pauper or vagrant shall remain in the city.

No person shall bring paupers or vagrants to the city.

§ 273.—Every slave or free negro, who shall violate the foregoing section, shall receive not exceeding fifty lashes.

Slaves or free negroes violating foregoing section.

§ 274.—Every pauper, vagrant, and idle or disorderly person of evil life, or ill fame; every person, who has no fixed place of residence, and no visible means of support, and every person, who begs or loiters about the streets or other public places, shall be arrested, and carried before the Mayor, who shall order him or her to leave the city, and if, at the expiration of twenty-four hours thereafter, such person shall be found in the city, he or she shall be fined not exceeding fifty dollars.

All paupers and evil persons sh'll be taken before the Mayor.

CHAPTER XXII.

POLICE, PATROL AND PRISONS.

Th police of the city.

§ 275.—The police force of the city shall consist of the City Marshal, Deputy Marshal, and as many assistant policemen as the City Council may deem necessary to elect.

The City Council sh'll elect a marshal.

§ 276.—The City Council, at its first meeting in every year, shall elect a city marshal, who shall receive a salary and continue in office for the term of one year.

The oath of the marshal

§ 277.—Before entering upon the duties of his office, the marshal shall make and subscribe the following affidavit, which shall be filed with the city clerk ; "I —— do solemnly swear or affirm that I will well and truly discharge the duties of marshall according to the laws of the city to the best of my ability."

The bond of the marshal.

§ 278.—The marshal, immediately after his election shall give a bond with sureties, which shall be filed with the city clerk, in the sum of one thousand dollars for the faithful performance of his duties. $500

The marshal shall patrol the streets, &c.

§ 279.—The marshal shall patrol the streets at all reasonable hours, preserve the peace, and arrest all persons, violating any law of the city.

The marshal shall execute all processes.

§ 280.—The marshal shall execute every summons or process, issued by the City Council, or the Mayor, or under the authority of the Mayor or City Council.

All persons shall assist the marshal

§ 281.—The marshal may command the citizens to aid him in the enforcement of the laws, or in the arrest of persons, violating the laws of the city, and any person, refusing to give such assistance, shall on conviction before the Mayor or an Alderman, be fined in the sum of ten dollars.

§ 282.—The marshal shall examine the streets, report their condition and superintend public works when required to do so, by the City Council ; he shall also act as clerk of the market, whenever that office shall be vacant.

The Marshal shall examine the streets.

§ 283.—The marshal shall have the market bell rang at nine o'clock, P. M., and see that the watchmen perform their duties, according to the laws of the city.

The Marshal shall have the market bell rang.

§ 284.—The City Council shall designate one of the persons elected, as the captain of the police ; and all the policemen shall take an oath for the faithful performance of their duties.

Captain of Police.

§ 285.—No person not a permanent resident in the city, shall be elected a policeman.

Policemen.

§ 286.—The policemen shall be under the control of the marshal, and shall assist him at all times to enforce the laws of the city. They shall act as watchmen at night, and perform such duties as may be required, and shall receive each month for their services such compensation as the City Council may appoint.

Policemen under command of the Marshal.

§ 287.—The marshal shall communicate his orders to the captain of the police, and require him to report daily the conduct of the men under his command ; and the marshal shall forthwith report all cases of neglect of duty to the Mayor or City Council.

Captain of Police shall report daily

§ 288.—The Mayor shall, from time to time, instruct the policemen as to their duties under the laws of the city.

Instructions of the policemen.

78

§ 289.—The marshal shall keep an account of the time any policeman under his control, fails to perform his duties, and during the time of such negligence or absence from his post, he shall receive no wages.

Policemen shall receive no wages when absent.

§ 290.—The policemen, acting as watchmen, shall arrest all suspicious and disorderly persons, and commit them to the guard-house or keep them in custody till morning, when they shall be carried before the Mayor or an Alderman, and be punished according to the provisions of the law they may have violated.

Suspicious persons.

§ 291.—The policemen shall enter any place where they suspect slaves or free negroes resort to gamble or drink, and shall arrest all disorderly slaves or any slave absent from his or her owner's or master's lot without permission, after half-past nine o'clock, P. M., and commit them to the guard-house until morning.

Slaves to gamble or drink, &c.

§ 292.—Every person, who shall forcibly resist the marshal, or any policeman in the discharge of his duty, shall be fined not less than twenty, nor more than fifty dollars, and in default of payment of the fine, he shall be committed to the guard-house until such fine is paid, but in no case shall such imprisonment exceed thirty days.

No person shall resist an officer.

§ 293.—Any persons, who shall interfere or attempt to interfere with the marshal or a policeman in the discharge of his duty ; or shall attempt to rescue a person, arrested by an officer of the city ; or shall assist a person to escape from custody, shall be fined not less than ten, nor more than twenty dollars·

§ 294.—Whenever the City Council, shall deem it proper, the city clerk shall enroll all the male citizens, between the ages of eighteen and forty-five years, who shall constitute the patrol guard.

Patrol, &c.

§ 295.—The names of the persons enrolled, shall be placed in a box on separate pieces of paper, and as many names daily drawn therefrom by the Mayor or an Alderman, as may be necessary for a patrol the ensuing night; and if any person whose name shall be drawn be absent, or objectionable, such name shall be returned to the box, to be drawn when the person can serve.

Names of persons enrolled.

§ 296.—The Mayor or Alderman drawing the patrol for any night, shall make a list of the names, state the time and place of the meeting of the patrol, and sign his name to it.

List of the persons drawn.

§ 297.—The marshal or a policeman, shall notify the persons constituting the patrol, at least five hours before the time of meeting; and any person having neither an excuse nor providing a substitute, who shall fail to appear and serve, shall be fined two dollars and costs.

Notifying the person drawn.

§ 298.—The person drawing the patrol, shall appoint one from the number drawn, to act as captain, who shall command the patrol, and report any one of the patrol for neglect of duty, disobedience of orders or for riotous and disorderly conduct.

The patrol shall appoint a captain, &c.

§ 299.—Any person, who shall fail or refuse without a good excuse to act as captain when appointed by the Mayor or an Alderman, shall, on conviction, be fined five dollars.

No person appointed captain sh'll refuse to act

§ 300.—Every one of the patrol, reported for neglect of duty, disobedience or disorderly conduct, shall, on conviction, be fined five dollars.

Neglect of duty.

§ 301.—The patrol shall walk through the streets during the whole night for which they were appointed, preserve good order and arrest all persons, disturbing the peace of the city, and shall have the authority, and perform all the duties of

Patrollers shall patrol the street.

the regular policemen, and any person failing to do so, shall on conviction, be fined five dollars.

Persons imprisoned in t h e guard house.

§ 302.—All persons committed to prison by the Mayor or an Alderman, by the marshal or captain of the police or patrol, shall be imprisoned in the guard-house, unless the Mayor or an Alderman shall, by special warrant in writing, otherwise direct.

The marshal shall rec've ten dollars for every arrest, &c.

§ 303.—The marshal shall have charge of the city prisons, and of the persons imprisoned therein, and shall receive two dollars for every arrest and commitment to prison; but if the person arrested be acquitted, the marshal shall receive nothing.

Removal of officers of city.

§ 304.—The City Council shall have the power to remove any officer of the city.

City officers purchasing, city Sheriff, &c.

§ 305.—Any officer, who shall purchase city scrip or warrants; or shall loan or use, on his own account, money belonging to the city; or shall directly or indirectly buy any property sold by the city clerk, or by any other person on account of taxes due the city may, according to the discretion of the City Council, be removed from office.

CHAPTER XXIII.

RETAILERS.

Retailers of spirituous liquors.

§ 306.—Every person, who shall retail spirituous or vinous liquors in a less quantity than one quart, or suffer it to be drank on his or her premises without obtaining a license from the City Council, for which five hundred dollars shall be paid, shall be fined not less than twenty-five, nor more than fifty dollars for each offence.

§ 307.—Every person, who shall retail porter, ale, or lager beer in a less quantity than one quart, or suffer it to be drank on his or her premises without a license granted by the City Council, for which two hundred and fifty dollars shall be paid, shall be fined not less than twenty-five, nor more than fifty dollars for each offence.

Retailers of ale beer, &c. must obtain a license.

§ 308.—The applicant, before obtaining his license, shall take and subscribe before the Mayor or an Alderman the following affidavit: "I —— do solemnly swear that I will not sell any vinous, spirituous or malt liquors to, or sell to, or purchase from, any slave any article or commodity without the permission of the owner, master or overseer of such slave; and that I will not knowingly suffer the same to be done by my partner, or clerk, agent, or any other person, upon, or about my premises, if in my power to prevent the same, and I will not allow any gaming of any kind to be carried on, on or about my premises, if in my power to prevent the same; and I will not violate directly or indirectly, by resorting to any device, or permit on my premises the violation of the laws of the city in relation to retailers." The affidavit must be filed in the office of the city clerk.

The oath of the applicant for a license.

§ 309.—Every license, issued to any person to retail spirituous, vinous, or malt liquors in a less quantity than one quart, must describe the house or place in which the business will be carried on, and must set forth the name of the person to whom the license was issued: and for any other place or person, the license shall be void.

License must describe the place, &c.

§ 310.—No license, granted to a retailer of spirituous, or vinous or malt liquors, shall be transferred; nor shall any person retail spirituous, vinous, or malt liquors in two places under one license; any

No license can be transferred, &c.

11

person violating this section, shall be fined fifty dollars.

§ 311.—Any retailer of spirituous, vinous, or malt liquors, or keeper of a public house, who shall permit gaming of any kind contrary to the laws of the State on his or her premises, shall be fined fifty dollars.

A retailer permitting gaming.

§ 312.—The City Council shall revoke the license of a retailer, who shall be convicted of selling liquor to slaves, or permitting slaves or free negroes to gamble on his, or her premises.

A retailer selling liquor to slaves.

§ 313.—Every retailer of spirituous, vinous or malt liquors, who shall permit any person on his premises, by loud singing, shouting or riotous conduct, or in any manner to disturb the neighbors, shall be fined not less than ten nor more than fifty dollars.

No retailer of liquors shall permit riotous conduct.

§ 314.—Every retailer, who shall permit gambling on his premises, or who shall sell, or in any manner dispose of spirituous, vinous or malt liquors, or any other article on the Sabbath, shall be fined not less than ten nor more than fifty dollars for each offence.

No retailer shall permit gambling, nor sell any article on the Sabbath.

§ 315.—The license of any retailer, violating either of the two preceding sections may be annulled by the City Council.

License of a retailer annulled.

§ 316.—Every house in which spirituous, vinous or malt liquors are sold, retailed, or given away, which is habitually resorted to by slaves or free negroes, or about which, slaves or free negroes assemble or loiter, shall be considered a public nuisance.

Shops where liquors are sold, and to which slaves or free negroes resort

§ 317.—Any person, keeping such a house, shall be fined fifty dollars on the first conviction of the offence, and if convicted the second time of the offence, shall not only be fined fifty dollars, but shall forfeit the license granted.

The keeper of such a house shall be fined.

§ 318.—No conviction of the offence defined and punished in the two foregoing sections, shall be suffered, unless evidence is given by three or more respectable witnesses, that the reputation of the house, or the keeper thereof, for illegally trading with slaves, is bad.

CHAPTER XXIV.

SLAVES AND FREE NEGROES.

§ 319.—Every slave, who shall reside or sleep in any enclosure, dwelling-house or other building not upon the premises occupied by the owner, agent or person representing the owner of such slave, shall on conviction receive thirty-nine lashes, unless the owner or his representative, will pay a fine of five dollars.

No slave shall reside or sleep in an enclosure apart from the owner, &c.

§ 320.—Every owner, or employer, or person representing the owner of a slave, who shall permit such slave to reside or sleep on premises contrary to the provisions of the preceding section, shall, on the first conviction of having violated the said section be fined not less than ten, nor more than fifteen dollars, and on every subsequent conviction, five dollars for each day the violation of the law shall continue.

No owner or employer of a slave shall permit him to sleep away from his lot.

§ 321.—Every person, who shall let, or rent a lot, house or room to a slave, within the limits of the city, shall be fined not exceeding fifty dollars, for each offence.

No person shall rent a lot or house to a slave.

§ 322.—Every slave, or free negro, who shall keep a shop or stall for the sale of beer, cakes,

No slave or free negro shall keep a

shop or stall.
fruit, soda water or any other article, on his or her own account, or for the benefit of another person, shall on conviction, receive not more than thirty-nine lashes, and shall be imprisoned till the officer's fees are paid.

Slaves or free negroes may keep a barber shop.
§ 323.—But nothing in this chapter shall be so construed as to prevent a slave or free negro, from keeping a barber shop, provided a license be obtained from the Mayor, for which ten dollars shall be paid for each person employed in the shop as a barber.

No person controlling a slave shall permit such slave to keep a shop or stall.
§ 324.—Any person, having control of a slave, who shall permit such slave to keep a shop or stall for any purpose whatever, shall, on conviction, be fined in any sum not less than ten, nor more than fifty dollars.

No person shall hire a slave by the day unless licensed.
§ 325.—Every person, who shall hire or employ a slave to work by the day, who is not regularly licensed by the Mayor, shall be fined not exceeding five dollars.

No person shall be permitted to work without a license.
§ 326.—Every person, having the control of a slave, who shall permit such slave to work by the day for wages, or to hire his or her own time, without a license from the Mayor, shall be fined not exceeding twenty dollars.

Slave caught off owner's lot.
§ 327.—Every slave caught at night off the premises of the owner, master, or person representing the owner of such slave, without a written permission, thirty minutes after the ringing of the nine o'clock bell, shall be punished by the marshal, with not more than twenty stripes, or be confined in the guard-house till morning.

The owner shall be informed of his imprisonment.
§ 328.—The marshal, at an early hour of the day, shall inform the owner or his agent of the confinement of the slave, and upon the payment of one dollar to the marshal for the use of the city, the slave shall be released, if the owner or agent

refuse to pay the marshal one dollar, as aforesaid, the slave shall receive not exceeding twenty stripes, and be discharged.

§ 329.—If the owner, or employer of the slave be a non-resident of the city, the marshal shall confine the slave for forty-eight hours in the guard-house, and receive the same rates for feeding the slave, that is allowed to the jailor of the county. Upon the expiration of forty-eight hours, unless some person controlling the slave appears and claims him or her, the slave shall be committed by the marshal as a runaway, to the county jail.

If the owner be a non-resident the marshal shall place the slave in jail.

§ 330.—Every slave, who shall own a cart, dray, or other vehicle, a horse, mare, gelding, mule, ox, hog, or dog, within the limits of the city, shall, on conviction, be punished with not more than thirty-nine stripes, unless the owner or person controlling the slave will pay a fine of ten dollars for each offence.

No slave shall own a dray. &c.

§ 331.—Any person, controlling a slave, who shall permit such slave to keep a horse, mare, gelding, mule or ox, within the limits of the city, shall be fined ten dollars, for each offence.

Any person controlling a slave shall not permit him to keep a horse.

§ 332.—Every slave or free negro, who shall fight, quarrel, use abusive, indecent or profane language, or act in an indecent manner in the view or hearing of a white person, within the limits of the city, shall, on conviction, receive any number of lashes not exceeding fifty. But this penalty may be avoided by the payment of any sum not exceeding fifty dollars, according to the discretion of the Mayor or Alderman, before whom the offender may be carried.

No negro shall fight or use indecent language.

§ 333.—Every slave or free negro, who shall bet at cards or dice, or play any game at which money

No negro shall gamble.

or any article of value is wagered, shall, on conviction, receive not exceeding fifty lashes.

No slave shall be present whenothers gamble.

§ 334.—Every slave or free negro, who is present where slaves or free negroes are playing at any game for money, or any other valuable article, shall, on conviction, be punished with not more than thirty-nine stripes.

No white personshall be present where negroes gamble.

§ 335.—Every white person, who shall be present where slaves or free negroes are playing at any game for money or other valuable property, shall, on conviction, be fined not less than twenty-five, nor more than fifty dollars.

Any negro who shall smoke in the streets, &c.

§ 336.—Every slave or free negro, who shall smoke a pipe or cigar in the streets, or carry a club, stick, or any kind of weapon, shall, on conviction, be punished with not exceeding one hundred stripes.

No negro shall harbor a runaway slave.

§ 337.—Every slave or free negro, who shall conceal or harbor a slave or write or furnish a pass or "free papers" to a slave, shall, on conviction, be punished with not exceeding fifty lashes on the bare back.

Slaves may be licensed to work by the day.

§ 338.—On the application of a citizen who is the owner of the slave, the Mayor shall grant a license to such slave to hire his own time by the day, for the purpose of cutting or sawing wood, and sweeping or cleaning bed-rooms and offices, and doing such other jobs as may add to the comfort of the citizens.

License for negroes.

§ 339.—On the payment of five dollars for a washer-woman, and ten dollars for any other laborer, the owner shall receive a badge with the number of the license, engraved or painted thereon, which shall be worn on a conspicuous part of the slave's dress.

§. 340.—The Mayor shall not grant license for a slave unless upon proof of the slave's good moral character ; and any slave wearing the badge of another, or using his or her own for a longer time than the license authorized, shall, on conviction, receive not exceeding thirty-nine stripes, unless the owner or person controlling the slave, will pay a fine of ten dollars.

No license shall be granted without proof of the slave's good character.

§ 341.—Every slave licensed to work by the day, who shall refuse to work for any white person, unless previously engaged or actually employed, shall receive not more than thirty-nine lashes, or the owner shall forfeit the license.

No licensed day-laborer shall refuse to work.

§ 342.—Every person, who having employed a licensed slave and shall fail or refuse to pay such slave after the work is finished, shall be fined not more than ten dollars.

Persons refusing to pay shall be fined.

§343 .—Every slave or free negro, who shall trespass on any lot or loiter about any private residence in the city without a good excuse, shall, on conviction, receive not less than ten nor more thirty-nine lashes.

No negro shall loiter about city.

§ 344.—Any assembly of slaves, without the permission of the City Council in which there shall be more than five negro men, not engaged in work or under the control of their owner or manager, shall be unlawful, and each slave shall receive not exceeding thirty-nine stripes.

Unlawful assembly of slaves.

§ 345.—Every white person of suspicious character, or free negro, who shall be present at any unlawful assembly of slaves, shall, on conviction, be fined in the sum of thirty dollars, one half of which, shall be paid to the informer, and if there be no informer, then to the officer making the arrest.

No white person or free negro shall be present at an unlawful assembly.

§ 346.—Every person, who shall sell, or barter, or give to a slave, spirituous or vinous li-

No person shall trade with slaves

quors, or sell to, or barter or buy from a slave any article of merchandise, without permission in writing from the owner or manager of the slave, describing the article to be sold or bought, shall, on conviction, be fined fifty dollars, one half of which may be given to the informer, according to the discretion of the Mayor or Alderman trying the case.

§ 347.—Every slave, who shall violate the preceding section, shall, on conviction, be punished with not exceeding thirty-nine stripes unless the owner or manager of the slave will pay a fine of ten dollars.

§ 348.—The preceding section shall not be construed so as to prevent a slave from selling milk, butter, poultry, eggs, fish, fruit, vegetables and any table supplies under a general permission in writing from the owner or his or her agent.

§ 349.—Proof that a slave, having an article of traffic entered at night or on the Sabbath a place where spirituous, vinous, or malt liquors or merchandise is usually sold, and came out without it; or that immediately after coming out of such a place, the slave had any kind of liquor or merchandise, shall be considered *prima facie* evidence of illegal trading with such slave by the keeper of the place.

§ 350.—Every person who shall illegally purchase, or receive from a slave, cotton, corn, fodder, oats, wheat flour, meal, bacon, pork, or any similar articles, shall on conviction, be fined fifty dollars; one half of the fine may be paid to the informer, and if there be no informer, then to the officer making the arrest, or all of the fine shall be paid into the city treasury, according to the discretion of the Mayor or Alderman, before whom the case may be tried.

§ 351.—All slave traders, or persons buying or selling slaves on commission, who shall exhibit their slaves at or near the Court House or Market, or in any of the public thoroughfares of the city, unless exposed for public sale, shall be fined twenty dollars.

No slave trader shall exhibit near the Court House. &c.

§ 352.—Every slave trader, dealer in slaves, or person buying or selling slaves on commission, who shall sell or offer for sale a slave within the limits of the city, without a license, for which one hundred dollars shall be paid, shall, on conviction, be fined fifty dollars for each day this section shall be violated.

Every slave trader shall procure a license.

§ 353.—Every free negro, who shall come from another State, or from any part of this State, and remain in this city longer than twenty days, shall be fined on conviction twenty dollars.

No free negro, coming from a distance shall stay in the city.

§ 354.—The city clerk shall keep a book, alphabetically arranged, which shall contain the name, the age, place of nativity, the occupation and place of sleeping, of every free negro in the city.

The clerk shall keep a register of free negroes

§ 355.—The clerk shall collect a fee of fifty cents for registering every free negro, according to the provisions of the preceding section, and the further sum of fifty cents for registering any change of residence or place of sleeping.

Clerk's fee for registering free negroes.

§ 356.—Every free negro, who moves his place of sleeping within the limits of the city, and fails to go forthwith before the clerk and register the removal, and the place then occupied by him, or her, shall be fined ten dollars.

No free negro shall move his place of sleeping.

§ 357.—The marshal shall examine the book kept by the clerk, at least once in three months,

The marshal shall examine

12

visit the residence of the free negroes, and arrest any negro violating the laws of the city.

the book kept by the Clerk, &c.

Free negroes failing to register their names

§ 358.—Every free negro, who shall fail or refuse to register his, or her name, age, occupation, residence, or place of sleeping, shall, on conviction, be fined twenty-five dollars.

Free negroes to be taxed.

§ 359.—Every free male negro over fifteen and under fifty years of age shall pay an annual tax of ten dollars, and every free negro woman over fifteen and under fifty years of age, shall pay an annual tax of five dollars.

A free negro having no property with which to pay taxes.

§ 360.—Any free negro destitute of property, and failing to pay the said tax, shall be hired out by the marshal to any person who will pay the tax, and take the negro for the shortest time for his, or her labor.

No free negro shall be out after 9½ o'clock. P. M.

§ 361.—Every free negro, who shall be found in the streets after half-past nine o'clock at night, shall be fined five dollars; and in default of payment, shall receive not exceeding fifty lashes.

No free negro shall associate with slaves.

§ 362.—Every free negro, who shall associate with slaves in any house or lot within the limits of the city, without permission of the owner or manager of such slave, shall be fined five dollars.

A free negro not paying a fine.

§ 363.—Any free negro over the age of fifteen, failing to pay a fine imposed for the violation of any law of the city, may be imprisoned not exceeding sixty days, or be compelled to work on the streets at the rate of one dollar per day, until such fine is paid.

No free negro who is a non-resident shall work in the city without license.

§ 364.—Every free negro, residing out of the city, who shall work within its limits without a license, for which the sum of twenty dollars shall be paid, shall be fined five dollars, for each offence.

CHAPTER XXV.

STREETS AND SIDEWALKS.

§ 365.—Every person who shall erect, or extend, or enlarge a house or building, or extend a fence so as to encroach upon the streets or sidewalks of the city, shall be fined ten dollars for every day such obstruction or encroachment shall continue, after being notified by an officer to remove it.

No person shall encroach on the sidewalks.

§ 366.—Every owner, agent or claimant of a lot in the city, who shall fail to make and keep in good repair a sidewalk on the whole length of such property, of the following width, viz : on streets over sixty and less than one hundred feet broad, a sidewalk twelve feet wide ; on streets more than one hundred feet in breadth, a sidewalk fourteen feet wide, exclusive of the gutters, shall be fined twenty dollars.

Every owner of a lot failing to make or keep in repair the sidewalk.

§ 367.—No person shall be compelled to repair the sidewalks adjoining his property, except in obedience to an order for that purpose, passed by the City Council.

City Council shall order the repairing of sidewalks.

§ 368.—Every person, who shall encumber a street or sidewalk with goods or merchandise, lumber, or fuel, or any article whatever, or with a carriage, wagon or other vehicle not in immediate use, for a longer time than is absolutely necessary, shall be fined ten dollars.

Any person encumbering street or sidewalk with any article, &c.

369.—The preceding section shall not be so construed as to deny any person for the purpose of building, the right to occupy one-third of the street in front of his or her lot for forty days.

How the preceding section shall be construed.

§ 370.—When any person shall fail to repair the sidewalk by his or her lot for five days after the City Council shall order it to be done, the sidewalk

When a person fails to repair his or her sidewalk.

shall be put in good order by the street hands, and the cost thereof shall be charged to the owner, and collected from him by the marshal upon the completion of the work.

No occupant of a house shall throw filth into the street.

§ 371.—Every occupant of a house or tenament, who shall throw filthy water, or fluids of any description from such house or tenament into the streets or sidewalks, shall be fined five dollars, for each offence.

No person shall deposit offensive matter in the street.

§ 372.—Every person, who shall throw or deposit offal or other offensive matter in the streets, except at the intersection thereof, shall be fined five dollars.

Streets excepted from foregoing section.

§ 373.—The provisions of the preceding sections, shall not apply to Market street, west of the Capitol, nor to Commerce street, nor to Lawrence, Perry and Court streets between Washington and the north side of Monroe street.

Height of cellar doors.

§ 374.—Every person, who shall build a cellar door above the level of the side walk, shall be fined five dollars, and one dollar for every day thereafter the cellar door shall remain higher than the sidewalk.

No person shall erect steps across sidewalk.

§ 375.—Every person who shall without the consent of the City Council erect steps on a sidewalk, shall be fined ten dollars.

No person shall obstruct the sewers.

§ 376.—Every person, who shall obstruct the gutters or sewers of the city with dirt, trash, wood, lumber, brick or other material, shall be fined five dollars.

No horse shall be fastened near the sidewalk.

§ 377.—Every person, who shall tie or fasten a horse in such a manner as to permit it to stand upon the sidewalk, shall be fined five dollars.

Any horse found on

§ 378.—Any horse found upon the sidewalk in violation of the preceding section, shall be seized and detained by the city marshal until the fine is paid. *(sidewalk shall be seized.)*

§ 379.—Every person, who shall ride, drive, or lead a horse on a sidewalk, shall be fined five dollars; but this shall not be so construed as to prevent a person from riding or driving across any part of a sidewalk used for the purpose. *(No person shall ride or drive on sidewalks.)*

§ 380.—Every person, who shall make a privy within four feet of a sidewalk, or within two feet of his boundary line (unless by consent of the proprietor of the adjoining lot,) shall be fined five dollars; and on failure to remove the privy, or on a second conviction of the offence, he shall be fined five dollars for each day it shall remain. *(No privy shall be built within four feet of the sidewalk.)*

§ 381.—Any person, who shall camp at night on a street or on any public grounds within the limits of the city, shall be fined five dollars for each night of such encampment. *(No person shall camp on the street or any public ground.)*

§ 382.—The provisions of the preceding section, shall not apply to persons camping on the banks of the river with the intention of leaving the city on a boat. *(Persons about to embark on boats not affected by preceding section.)*

§ 383.—Every person, who shall fly a kite within the limits of the city, shall be fined five dollars; and every slave or free negro, violating this section shall receive not exceeding twenty lashes. *(Persons flying kites shall be fined.)*

CHAPTER XXVI.

TREASURER, TAX ASSESSORS AND TAXES.

§ 384.—The City Council shall elect annually a Treasurer, who shall take an oath to discharge faithfully the duties of this office. *(The City Council shall annually elect a Treasurer.)*

§ 385.—The city treasurer, before entering upon the duties of his office, shall make a bond for such sum as the City Council may require, with good sureties, approved by the City Council, for the performance of his duties, and the custody of all money or papers received by him.

The City Treasurer shall give a bond.

§ 386.—The Treasurer shall receive all money belonging to the city, and state from whom and when obtained, and whether it be derived from taxes, fines or licenses, or any other source, and pay out money only under an order of the City Council, passed in open council upon the certificate of the clerk.

The Treasurer shall receive the money belonging to the city, &c

§ 387.—The Treasurer at the first meeting of the City Council, in every month, shall render an account of all the money received and paid out by him, with written vouchers to sustain credits claimed by him.

The Treasurer shall make reports monthly.

§ 388.—The account of the Treasurer after being approved by the City Council, shall be recorded by the clerk, and the account and vouchers filed in his office, every settlement so made shall be considered *prima facie* correct.

The account of the treasurer shall be filed with the clerk.

§ 389.—The City Council shall fix the salary of the treasurer prior to his election, and shall not diminish it during his term of office.

salary of the Treasurer.

§ 390.—The City Council, shall have full power to remove the treasurer at any time, the interest of the city requires his dismissal, and elect his successor.

The City Council has power to remove treasurer.

§ 391.— The City Council shall appoint, annually, three assessors of taxes, who shall be residents of the city.

Appointing of tax assessors.

§ 392.—The assessors, after being sworn to perform their duties faithfully, shall estimate the value of all real estate in the city according to their judgment, and report such valuation to the Mayor on or before the first day of July in each year, unless further time shall be granted by the City Council.

The assessors shall make reports.

§ 393.—The assessors having made their return, the Mayor shall lay it before the City Council, and give ten days' notice of the assessment, and in such printed notice, he shall also appoint a time for hearing and determining all complaints against the action of the assessors.

The Mayor shall give notice of the assessment, &c.

§ 394.—At the time appointed for hearing objections against the valuation made by the assessors, all errors and omissions shall be corrected and supplied by the City Council, and the assessment when approved and the tax laid thereon, shall create a lien on the property for the taxes of the current year.

The assessment shall create a lien on the property, &c.

§ 395.—The taxes, assessed by the authority of the City Council, shall be collected by the city clerk.

Collection of taxes.

§ 396.—On the application of the clerk, the Mayor shall issue an execution after the first day of March in every year, against any property owned by a person, who shall neglect to pay the tax due from him or her on the last assessment; and the clerk shall levy the execution and collect the money due thereon.

The Mayor at request of clerk shall upon an execution, &c.

§ 397.—The clerk having levied an execution on personal property after advertising for ten successive days in a city newspaper, the property, the time and place of sale, shall sell the said property for cash at public auction before the Court-House door, or at the Artesian Basin, and apply the pro-

The clerk shall advertise the property, &c.

ceeds of the sale to the payment of the taxes due, together with all the costs incurred.

Sale of real estate advertised. § 398.—When the execution is levied on real estate, the owner of which is known, the clerk shall advertise in a city newspaper for thirty days the property, the time and place of sale, together with the amount of tax due thereon, and if the owner of the real estate be unknown, then the clerk shall publish such notice for ninety days.

The assessment *prima facie* evidence. § 399.—When taxes are assessed against real estate the owner of which is not known, the assessment shall be *prima facie* evidence that the owner is unknown.

Real estate sold for taxes may be redeemed. § 400.—Any lot, or subdivision of a lot, if separately assessed may be sold for taxes, and may be redeemed by the owner, or his, or her agent at any time within two years from the sale, upon the payment to the purchaser, or to the city treasurer for him, four times the amount of taxes, costs and expenses, paid by the purchaser, and interest at the rate of twenty per cent. per annum, on all the purchase money over and above the taxes, costs, and expenses of such sale.

The proceeds of property sold for taxes. § 401.—The proceeds of the sale, exceeding the taxes, interest, costs, and expenses, shall be paid into the city treasury for the owner, and the treasurer shall be responsible on his official bond for the safe custody of them.

City Council may purchase real estate sold for taxes. § 402.—The City Council, by its agent, may purchase real estate, sold for taxes, and the conveyance of it shall be made to the Mayor for the use of the city. The real estate so purchased by the city, shall be subject to redemption, as in other cases, and when redeemed, shall be conveyed by the Mayor to the original owner.

§ 403.—All sales shall be made before the Court-House door, or at the Artesian Basin in Court square. *The place of sales.*

§ 404.—Every person, who shall pay the tax assessed against his or her property prior to the first day of December next after the assessment, shall be entitled to a reduction of interest from the payment till the first day of December, and every person who shall fail to pay the tax on the first day of December, shall pay interest on the amount of taxes due, from that time until the tax shall be paid. *Persons paying taxes prior to first of December. Persons failing to pay tax on first December.*

§ 405.—Every lawyer, doctor, and dentist, shall pay an annual tax of five dollars. *Lawyers, Doctors, & Dentists.*

§ 406.—Every daguerreotypist, ambrotypist or artist of like character shall pay an annual tax of five dollars. *Daguerreotypsit.*

§ 407.—All gold watches shall be taxed fifty cents, and all gold watch-chains, twenty-five cents; all silver watches and all clocks shall be taxed twenty-five cents. *Gold watches and chains.*

§ 408.—All furniture, silver ware, and silver plated ware over the value of five hundred dollars, shall be taxed annually one quarter of one per cent. on its value. *All furniture, silver wares, &c.*

§ 409.—Every white man between the ages of twenty-one, and fifty years, shall be taxed two dollars. *All white men taxed.*

§ 410.—Every saddle or carriage horse shall be taxed one dollar, and every pleasure carriage one per cent. on its value. *Saddle or carriage horses and carriages taxed.*

§ 411.—Every slave over ten and under fifteen years of age, shall be taxed fifty cents, and every slave over fifteen and under fifty years of age, shall be taxed one dollar. *Slaves shall be taxed.*

CHAPTER XXVII.

VOTERS.

Illegal voting.

§ 412.—Every person who shall vote illegally at any election for Mayor, aldermen or clerk of the city, shall be fined fifty dollars.

CHAPTER XXVIII.

WHARFINGER, WHARFAGE AND WHAVES.

Election of wharfinger.

§ 413.—The City Council shall elect annually a wharfinger, and fix his salary, which shall neither be increased nor diminished during his term of office.

The wharfinger shall make oath.

§ 414.—The wharfinger, before entering upon the duties of his office, shall make the following affidavit, which shall be filed with the clerk; "I do solemnly swear or affirm that I will discharge the duties of wharfinger of the city of Montgomery, to the best of my ability, and will be diligent in assessing and collecting wharfage due the city."

The wharfinger shall give bond.

§ 415.—The wharfinger shall also give a bond of ten thousand dollars, with sufficient sureties for the faithful performance of his duties, and for the payment to the treasurer under the direction of the City Council, of all money or property of any kind, belonging to the city.

The wharfinger shall keep a book, &c.

§ 416.—The wharfinger, shall keep a book, in which shall be entered the wharfage, collected each day, the amount paid upon each article, and the name of the person by whom it was paid ; and the said book shall be subject to the inspection of the Mayor or an Alderman at all times, and on the resignation or removal of the wharfinger, he shall deliver the book to the City Council.

§ 417.—The wharfinger, shall render an account at the first meeting of the City Council, in every month, and oftener if required by the City Council, in which, he shall state the money received by him, and the amount paid over to the treasurer under the direction of the City Council.

The wharfinger shall make a quarterly report.

§ 418.—The wharfinger, shall report to the Council what repairs are needed on the wharf. He shall settle all disputes in relation to places upon it, and have a general control, and superintendence of it for the interest of the city.

The wharfinger shall report what repairs are needed, on the wharf.

§ 419.—All goods, wares, and merchandise, cotton, lumber, brick, stock and all things whatever, shipped from or landed on, the city wharf, shall be subject to the following rates of wharfage, viz :

Rates of wharfage.

For each bale of cotton,	$0,08
" " barrel,	05
" " sack of coffee,	03
" " " " salt,	03
" " " " grain,	03
" hogshead or pipe,	02
" hundred weight of any metal,	$02\frac{1}{2}$
" buggy or sulky,	75
" carriage,	1,00
" thousand feet lumber,	50
" horse or cow,	10
" sheep or hog,	$02\frac{1}{2}$

Boxes, packages, or merchandise at the rate of one cent. per square foot. All other articles shall pay at the above rates, and according to weight and measurement.

The duty of wharfinger.

§ 420.—The wharfinger shall have a lien upon all articles, and every species of property subject to wharfage, landed on, or shipped from, the city wharf, and shall retain possession of such articles or property until the wharfage is paid.

No person shall receive merchandise on the Sabbath.

§ 421.—Every person, who shall, on the Sabbath, receive or deliver on the wharf, or at any place within the limits of the city. bales of cotton, produce, goods, wares, and merchandise, or stock of any kind, shall, on conviction, be fined fifty dollars.

Tax on all boats at the wharf.

§ 422.—The wharfinger, shall demand of the owner or person having charge of a steamboat five dollars, and of the owner or person controlling a barge, flat-boat, or any boat carrying freight, two dollars for every day such boat may be at the city wharf.

Any person refusing to pay tax.

§ 423.—Any person having a boat at the wharf, and refusing to pay the tax mentioned in the preceding section, shall be fined ten dollars in addition to the tax, due on such boat.

Persons refusing to pay the above tax shall be arrested.

§ 424.—The marshal upon being notified by the wharfinger of such a person's refusal to pay the tax, due upon a boat, shall take such person before the Mayor or an Alderman, and shall receive from the delinquent two dollars for making the arrest.

Removing gravel, &c., from the wharf.

§ 425.—Every person who shall remove rocks, pebbles, or gravel from the city wharves, shall be fined five dollars for each offence.

APPENDIX.

AN ORDINANCE.

TO PROVIDE FOR LIGHTING THE CITY OF MONTGOMERY
WITH GAS.

SECTION 1.—*Be it ordained by the City Council of Montgomery*, That from and after the passage of this ordinance, the exclusive privilege shall be, and the same is hereby granted for the term of fifty years from the first day of November, A. D., 1852, to John Jeffrey & Co., of Cincinnati, Ohio, their associates successors and assigns of laying pipes for conducting gas under any street, alley, or thoroughfare within the corporate limits of the city : *Provided*, that the said pipes shall be so laid as not to interfere with the drainage or sewerage or the grade of any street, alley or thoroughfare in said city ; and *Provided*, that if any changes or alterations in the drainage, sewerage or grade of any street, alley or thoroughfare shall be made by order of the City Council, which shall render a change or alteration necessary in the position of said gas pipes, the expense of all such changes and alterations shall be paid by the City Council of Montgomery.

The privilege of lighting the city with gas granted to John Jeffrey & Co.

Proviso.

SEC. 2.—That the privilege herein granted is upon the condition that the said John Jeffrey & Co., shall, on or before the first day of May, A. D., 1854, have completed the requisite apparatus for

The apparatus for the manufacture of gas shall be completed, and three

manufacturing gas, and shall have laid in connection therewith three miles of main pipe in the streets of Montgomery, and shall further lay from time to time such additional main pipes in any street, alley, or thoughfare as shall be required by the said City Council ; *Provided*, that the demand for gas to be supplied by such extension shall afford a reasonable prospect for a fair remuneration.

Sec. 3.—That the gas works shall not be erected within one hundred yards of any habitation within the corporate limits of the city, without the consent of the owners thereof, and the operations of said gas works, shall be so conducted as not to occasion injury to the health or comfort of the inhabitants of the city.

Sec. 4.—That whenever the said John Jeffrey & Co., desire to break ground in any street, alley, or thoroughfare for the purpose of laying pipes, they shall give at least three day's notice thereof to the Mayor or marshal of the city, and during the progress of the work, they shall not unnecessarily obstruct or incumber said street, alley, or thoroughfare, and shall proceed with all reasonable diligence to complete the work, and when the pipes are laid they shall repair the street, alley, or thoroughfare in such manner as shall be approved by the said Mayor or marshal of the city.

Sec. 5.—That the said John Jeffrey & Co., and their associates, successors and assigns shall, from time to time, and at all times furnish to the city of Montgomery, for the public use and benefit, such quantities of gas of the most approved quality for lighting cities, upon the several streets, alleys, and thoroughfares in which gas pipes shall be laid as may from time to time be required by said City Council, and for the gas furnished and consumed

for the public benefit as herein provided, the said
City Council will pay the said John Jeffrey &
Co., one-half of the price per cubic foot, at which
gas shall be furnished by them to the citizens ot
Montgomery for private consumption as hereinafter provided.   And all public lamps and lamp-posts,
and fittings, and fixtures thereto belonging, shall
be provided, and erected by the said John Jeffrey
& Co., at the expense of the said City Council,
and the necessary service pipes leading to, and con-
necting therewith shall be supplied and adjusted by,
and at the expense of the said John Jeffrey & Co.

Lamps and lamp-posts shall be provided at the expense of the city.

SEC. 6.—That the said John Jeffrey & Co., and
their associates, successors and assigns shall at all
times supply the inhabitants of the city of Montgomery for private use in the manner most approved
with a sufficient quantity of gas of the most approved quality at as low a price per cubic foot of
gas consumed, as the same quantity of gas shall be
furnished for the same purpose to the inhabitants
of any town or city, similarly situated, of equal or
greater population, than the city of Montgomery
in the Southern States, *Provided*, that the said
John Jeffrey & Co., shall not be required to provide gas as aforesaid for private consumption to
persons, whose premises are not within a reasonable
distance of a supply pipe already laid, nor to any
person who will not pay for gas monthly in advance
if so required, and *Provided*, further that the
said John Jeffrey & Co., may furnish gas to any
person for private use, at a distance from supply
pipes already laid, beyond what is contemplated in
this ordinance and may charge for gas so furnished
such additional price as may be agreed upon by the
contracting parties.

The citizens shall be sup plied with gas, &c.

Measurement of gas. SEC. 7.—That the amount of gas, consumed shall be ascertained by metre measurement in the usual way.

The City Council shall have the right to purchase the gas works. SEC. 8.—That at the expiration of twenty-five years from the first day of November, A. D., 1852, the City Council of Montgomery, shall have the right or privilege of purchasing from the said John Jeffrey & Co., and their associates, successors, and assigns, all the pipes, buildings and apparatus constituting the gas works at such a price as may be ascertained, and determined by five disinterested men, two of whom shall be chosen by the City Council of Montgomery, two by the said John Jeffrey & Co., and their associates, successors, and assigns, and the fifth by the four thus chosen.

An act of incorporation. SEC. 9.—It is understood that the said John Jeffrey & Co., will endeavor at the next session of the Legislature of Alabama to obtain an Act of incorporation in order to afford to such citizens as may desire, or to the City Council, the opportunity of becoming stockholders in the gas works herein comtemplated, to any extent not exceeding one-half of the entire stock.

When this ordinance shall take effect. SEC. 10.—That this ordinance shall take affect, and be binding upon the parties, so soon as the said John Jeffrey & Co., shall signify in writing their assent thereto.

Adopted by the board of Mayor and Aldermen, August 30th, 1852.

Concurred in by the board of Common Council, September 15th, 1852.

Approved October 13th, 1852.

SAMUEL D. HOLT, Mayor.

MONTGOMERY, ALABAMA,
October 4th, 1852.

We hereby assent to the terms and conditions of the foregoing ordinance for lighting the city of Montgomery with gas.

The assent of John Jeffrey & Co.

(Signed) JOHN JEFFREY & CO.,
By their Attorney in fact,
WASHINGTON BARROW,
of Nashville Tennessee.

AN ACT

The more effectually to secure the collection of rents in the City of Montgomery.

Proceedings upon oath of landlord or his agent.

SECTION 1.—*Be it enacted by the Senate and House of Representatives of the State of Alabama, in General Assembly, convened,* That whenever any landlord, his agent, or attorney, shall make complaint on oath to any justice of the peace in the city of Montgomery, that any person or persons is or are indebted to him for rent of any tenement within the corporate limits oi the said city, and shall enter into bond and security in four times the amount of the rent alleged to be due conditioned to pay the said defendant all costs and damages he may recover for the wrongful or vexatious suing out of the

Warrant issued, directed.

warrant hereinafter mentioned, it shall be lawful ior the said justice of the peace to issue his warrant returnable before him not less than four nor more than ten days from the time the warrant shall be issued, directed to any constable of said city requiring him to seize, and to take into his possession any goods and chattels belonging to the defendant, which may be found in the tenement for which the rent shall be due ; and the constable shall keep the goods and chattels so seized to answer the judgment which may be rendered by the justice of the peace in the cause unless the debt shall be sooner paid with all costs; and the justice of the peace on return of said warrant shall proceed, and render judgment according to the merits of the case.

SEC. 2.—*And be it further enacted,* That whenever the sum sworn to be due shall exceed the sum of fifty dollars, it shall be the duty of the justice of the peace to direct the same to the sheriff of the county of Montgomery, and make the same returnable before the county or Circuit Court of the said county, which Court shall proceed at the return term of said warrant to render judgment in the said cause; and it shall be the duty of the said sheriff of the said county, to proceed in the manner directed by the first section of this Act.

SEC. 3.—*And be it further enacted,* That the said defendant to the said warrant may replevy the property seized; *Provided,* he enter into bond and security payable to the plaintiff in double the amount of the sum sworn to be due, conditioned to pay the judgment which shall be rendered against him, or surrender the said property to the proper officer, and the said bond shall have the force and effect of a judgment, and execution may issue thereon, if the property so replevied shall not be delivered to the proper officer within fifteen days after the rendition of judgment. *(Defendant may replevy upon giving bond.)*

SEC. 4.—*And be it further enacted,* That if any shall wrongfully or vexatiously sue out such warrant, he shall be liable to pay the defendant therin treble damages to be recovered by action on the case before any court having competent jurisdiction. *(Penalty for wrongfully suing out warrant.)*

Approved, March 2d, 1848.

FORMS.

SUMMONS.

THE STATE OF ALABAMA, }
City of Montgomery.   }

To the Marshal of the City of Montgomery:

You are commanded to summon A. B. to appear before me on the............day of............1861, at the office of the Mayor, to answer to a charge of......................................
......................................when you will then and there make return of this summons.

C. D., Mayor.

Issued the.........day of..............1861.

A WARRANT OF ARREST.

THE STATE OF ALABAMA, }
City of Montgomery.   }

To the Marshal of the City of Montgomery:

Complaint having been made before me, that A. B. has committed the offence of..
....................................You are therefore commanded forthwith to arrest the said A. B., and bring him before me.

C. D., Mayor.

Issued the.........day of..............1861.

SUBPŒNA.

THE STATE OF ALABAMA, }
City of Montgomery. }

To the Marshal of the City of Montgomery:

You are hereby commanded to summon........................
personally to appear before the Mayor of the City of Montgomery, at.........on the..........day of............1861, and from
day to day thereafter, until discharged by due course of law,
to give evidence, and the truth to speak, in behalf of............
.........in a case now pending before the said Mayor, in which
the City Council of Montgomery is Plaintiff and.................
Defendant, and have you then and there this writ with your
endorsement thereon.

A. B., Clerk.

Issued the.........day of.............. 1861.

BAIL BOND.

THE STATE OF ALABAMA, }
City of Montgomery. }

We, A. B., C. D. and E. F., agree to pay the City of
Montgomery...............dollars, unless the said A. B. appear
before the Mayor on the.........day of.........1861, and from
day to day thereafter until discharged by law, to answer to
the offence of................... ....

Approved.

G. H. }

A. B. L. S.
C. D. L. S.
E. F. L. S.

APPEAL BOND.

THE STATE OF ALABAMA, ⎫
Montgomery County.   ⎬

Know all men by these presents, that we, A. B., C. D. and E. F., are held and firmly bound unto the City Council of Montgomery in the sum of.........dollars, well and truly to be paid to the said City Council of Montgomery.

Scaled with our seals. Dated the.........day of.........One Thousand Eight Hundred and Sixty-one.

The condition of the above obligation is such that if the said A. B. shall prosecute with effect an appeal by him, taken this day, from a judgment rendered against him for the sum of.........dollars, in favor of the City Council of Montgomery, before ...., Mayor of the City of Montgomery— to the next term of the Circuit Court of the said county, then the said obligation shall be void: But if said A. B. fail therein, then the said A. B., C. D. and E. F., shall pay the said judgment, with such damages, both of debt and costs, as shall be adjudged against the said A. B. in the said Court.

Scaled and delivered ⎫
in presence of........... ⎬   A. B.   L. S.
                         ⎭   C. D.   L. S.
                                    E. F.   L. S.

—

INDEX.

PAGE. SEC.

ANIMALS (*Continued.*)

	PAGE	SEC
Horses not allowed to run in the streets	32	30
Marshal shall advertise and sell horses	32	31
Owner may obtain the horse.............	32	32
Owner may prove title within one year	32	33
Horses must not be tied to public fences or lamp-posts....................	50	128
Persons permitting horses to stand on a side-walk, fined...............	92	377
Horses found on side-walk shall be siezed........................	92	378
Dogs, without collars, must not run at large........................	33	36
The Marshal must procure dog-collars	33	34
The Marshal must sell collars only to white persons....................	33	34
The Marshal shall register number of collar........................	33	35
The Marshal must not sell collars to slaves or free negroes....................	33	37
No slave shall keep a dog..............	33	38
Free negroes not to keep dogs without license........................	33	39
Cruelty to, punished......	47	112-14

APPEALS.

May be taken from decisions of the Mayor or an Alderman to City Council	30	20
May be taken from decision of the Mayor to the Circuit Court..............	19	

APPROPRIATIONS.

The Clerk shall keep an account of......	44	99

ARRESTS.

Warrant, form of....................	110	
Persons arrested may give bond...	29	18
Persons arrested may be imprisoned......	30	19

131

www.ingramcontent.com/pod-product-compliance
Lightning Source LLC
Chambersburg PA
CBHW020548270326
41927CB00006B/768